message
from the
vessel in
a dream

message

FROM

the

VESSEL

in

A

DREAM

Christopher Luna

FLOWSTONE PRESS

Collage art by Christopher Luna

Author photo (p. 130) by Julian Nelson
Back cover author photo by Cara Cottingham

The cover image was created by Christopher Luna
as an homage to the song "Thruster" by Outer Space Heaters
(https://outerspaceheaters.com)

First Flowstone Press Edition • November 2018
ISBN 978-1-945824-22-7

Dedicated with love and respect to
Carlos Santana,
the vessel in a dream who gifted me with the lines
"you make your appearance known/ through some creator."
This is the only time I have ever received poetry
from a dream.

TABLE OF CONTENTS

Launched into a Lifetime
of Mediated Experience

Abundant Fortune:
The Architecture of Poetic Vision

Fecund Labyrinth:
The Whole Impossibility of Actually Seeing Something

Collage Poetry: An Afterword

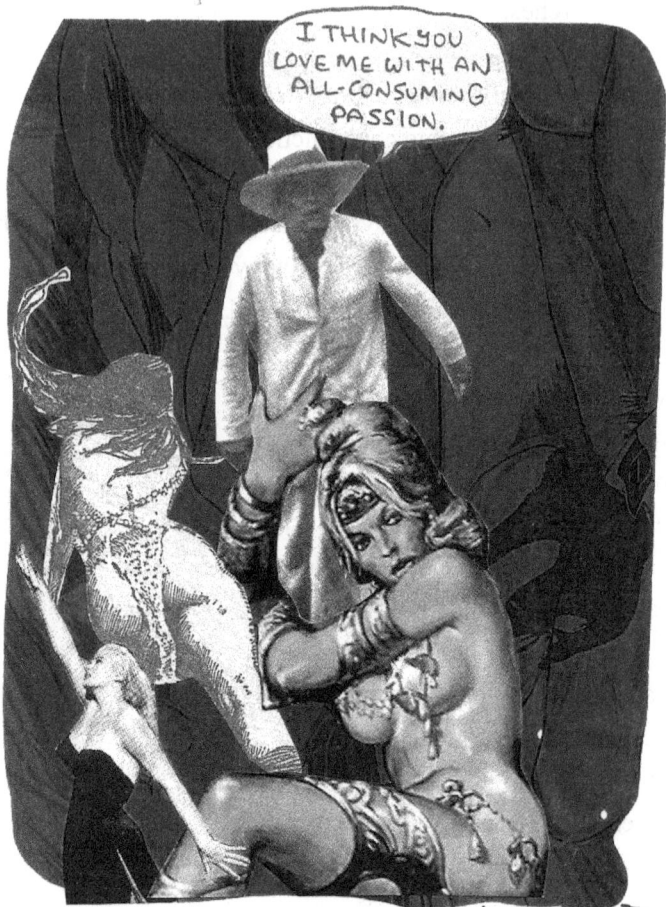

Stretching Toward humility
Sequence, Sometimes Metaphysical

Launched into a Lifetime of Mediated Experience
Rebecca Wolff

All beauty is at continuous war with God
Jack Spicer

I.

You've got It all wrong.
Whatever-It-Is
cannot be labeled, cornered, captured, or caged.
Its power comes
from the Mystery
Its Beauty the direct result
of Its Ineffability.
Not-Knowing is the secret.
Not-Needing to Know is the Key.
Realizing that the answer is unattainable
        And ought to remain that way.

You fuck things up
when you try to
place It in a box
        erect palaces
        build altars
        put it on display
        for all the world to see.
The Glory in Captivity.

II.

Not-Knowing can be painful, but it feels
more honest. Rather be in the dark with
Hope than standing in the Light, nothing
left to learn.

My disappointment is boundless. Your
pretty words would be easier to swallow
were they not so often followed by the
gleeful slitting of your brother's throat.

What, I ask you,
has any of this to do
with Love?

Magic happens when you least expect it

Nursery rhymes from the Gods. All you can eat porn.
Busy signal blues. Minute particulars speculum. We all
suffer from a certain crisis. A thick beauty. But it is pure
sound and much nonsense I think. Don't salivate all
                        over my hard-won
                                    preconceived notion

                        'tis a trigger I own

                                    Epiphany at every step.
                        Pretty amazing what can happen
                            when you organize your data.

daydreaming about
sending pictures
through the sky

                                            strung out on life,
                            strung out on your old lady,
                                or strung out on whatever

Every man prays in his own language.
There is no language that God does not understand.

    I get the majority of my news today from librarians and poets
                I'm a punk—that's what I do

Magic happens when you least expect it. Yugen Rashad.

Nursery rhymes from the Gods. But it is pure sound and nonsense I think. Poet Rob Sparks on Edgar Allan Poe.

Epiphany at every step. Czeslaw Milosz.

Strung out on life, strung out on your old lady, or strung out on whatever. Etta James, *Relix Magazine* September/October 2006.

Every man prays in his own language. There is no language that God does not understand. Duke Ellington.

I get the majority of my news today from librarians and poets. Eric Padget.

A rant for Sean Patrick Hill
(and any poet who'll listen)

1. Time spent sniffing elders arses may be necessary for the learned to have something to say at salons and dinner parties, but before we leave the ranters, the street cats, and the slang slingers behind in the literary remainder bin, take a moment to consider that ours is an oral tradition, however well-documented. This storyteller has seen/heard his share of loudmouthed no-talent shouters; nevertheless, I believe that a poet should go forth with all possible tools at his disposal—her postmodern sesh stuffed with rhyme, meter, philosophy, melody, gunfire, dialect, subway clack, Blaxploitation samples, vernacular, grid, spam, or mad-lib. There's a reason Whitman referred to them as songs. For a poet to declare himself "done with spoken word" is patently absurd, for without the word made flesh, without the thought made breath, there'd be no poesy at all.

enough of this elitist bull in F
Christ himself was one of the first slam poets
shouting his wild notions to any and all who would stop to listen
and not making a cent.   "angelheaded hipster" spawned
an entire belief system, not to mention centuries of madness and bloodshed

remember, it's the quiet ones you've gotta watch out for
the quiet ones   ("he seemed like such a nice boy")
who end up driving around with a body under a tarp in the back of their pickup
a little girl bound to a cot in a basement dungeon
or simmering human body parts in a crock pot

however marginalized we may feel
however devalued these words may be
it is absolutely crucial that we speak now

if for no other reason than
allowing history to record
that a few of us protested
the jackboot at the throat
of our glorious dream
                    democracy

2. we are lunatics who hope to lasso the inevitable, to
impose order on all that is beyond our understanding
or ability to control. been disabled, done forgivin'
the soul murderers, the glazed-eyed bitches who just
don't get it. and what is there to get? we are lunatics
who slap labels on metaphysics, moonlight, and
the nature of nature itself. impressed by our own
cleverness, satisfied to have established our own
superiority, we sit in coffeeshops and classrooms
smug, ears plugged, eyes sealed, open them again
and you shall be healed.

3. LOVING POETRY IS LIKE BEING A FAN OF HORROR MOVIES
             so enamoured with the genre
             that you are willing to sit through movies that are
                    completely moronic
                    and not-at-all scary
             in the hopes of catching
             that one unique concept
                    or cool character
             or original way of dispatching with someone
    (the basketball which completely obliterates a person's head
             in that piece of shit *Deadly Friend*
             or the fully grown adult male who claws
             his way out of the woman who has been raped
                    by an alien in *Xtro*)
             you stick with it to the end
                    because you love it

fully realizing that they can't all be
The Exorcist, *The Omen*, or
Night of the Living Dead
can't all be Cronenberg, Argento,
Lewton, Whale, or Carpenter
dig?

4. procrastinators recreate reciprocal feedback, angelfood cake, the perfect foot, perfectly bare, bouncing casually before my lustful stare, one typically Pacific Northwest flip-flop dangling from the toes I long to suckle and care for, 'cept she's an evacuee, and I'm a sultan trapped in a dimestore Buddha's body. this is just an aside. one side. of the story. this is just a glimpse of the perfectly full-of-shit narrative I've carefully devised to deflect attention from my growing belly. a pear is no object. "very well, then, I contradict myself, I contain multitudes." (Whitman) always wanted to be larger than life, like Morrison, Mingus, or Cinemascope. won't you wrap those beautiful arms around my habit-forming girth, break off some for a rationalization junkie "in chains of mind locked up?" (Blake)

5. she threw three baby Jesuses from the trestle into the San Francisco Bay. drowned her own flesh and it barely registered. scumbags like William Bennett will blame her DNA, while he and his brownshirts fuck the lower-class every day. painful to even glance at the columns anymore, but we must not turn away. it is time to reclaim the language in the service of noise, bliss, and revolution. ancient bards suffer from diminished expectation, unaware of the beauty in the truth revealed by their every exhalation. big guy knows what I'm talkin' about. griot gets it. ghetto rapper is aware. Cage was hip. Jungian slip

on the scientific tip
moronic design
but even after all
the blood
    she still fine

message from the vessel in a dream
no holds bar'd. tear it up –
s'got nothing to do with me.

Locked in the Get Right with God Room

It wasn't all doom and gloom in the insane asylum. You're too blessed to be stressed. I began by seeking an Answer. Only later did I realize that it is much more important to formulate the proper Question.

A righteous endeavor. A responsibility of the freethinking. A calling. The Messenger's path entails lifelong enrollment in a self-generated correspondence course entitled Society/ Symbolism/ Synchronicity.

Caught in The Black Balloon. Your time is done. You have done quite enough damage. I will emerge from the darkness to permeate the placenta of your ancient children's stories, tearing away at the protective membrane of your deeply-held convictions. Up is Down and Dark is Light. Chew my way out in my quest for The Light.

Inspired by an interview with artist Elizabeth McGrath published in *Juxtapoz Magazine*.

Stronger than dirt

Old rasta man at the top of the subway stairs. Everything slows down and shifts, like the scrambled eggs in your yesterday. These are the last days for the mischief makers.

Two black boys sit across from one another, one reading *The Scarlet Letter*, the other Edith Hamilton's *Mythology*. A young woman scribbles down notes on the back cover of *The Trial*. This does not necessarily make her smart.

Doubts spring forth unrelentingly. That dog is like a sundial chokin' on a spark. At 29 years he solved the mystery. The Clive Cussler/Jim Morrison connection revealed. My knees hurt, no not always. Where are you rushing to?

At seven months, when Angelo needed sleep, we put on the Wu. Father napped with him, and dreamed of a plague of vermin, some of which ballooned to the size of rabbits. The little ones snapped and bled between his fingers and burst under his feet.

"Can you remember before you were born? Can you remember that far back?" These documents are critical. Rubber bands strewn everywhere. Papercut mark of the self-aware criminal.

Your Lord Is A Traffic Cop

Diamonds are forever? Well so are mutilations. Stars in waiting line the subway platforms of NYC posing for magazine covers. These slaves speak a foreign tongue that defies interpretation, coded, branded, and supposed to death. Listen to the music in their exhalation. Reflection of the condescension inherent in your well-practiced presumption. What's the story behind those eyes? Lids heavy, what kind of trouble have they seen? Where have those hands been?

Channel Z (circa 1989)

suddenly static in my own time in your own
time beware a tear can appear a rip a slash
through the static in a moment and suddenly
too suddenly you are not wherever you are
but *then* again and there may be no reason
why but there you are in the lavender shorts
the garment that stuck around not wanting to
miss a moment of this crisis this chaos this
crisis of faith this fundamental fissure in the
unseen scripture you rarely regarded as worth
your time that time static that age static in my
attic laughs in a darkened kitchen and you did
not then and you do not now believe do not
believe do not believe in anything but love

Gardening. Very groovy. An adorably calf-like face. Art. Advertising. Not golf. He was terrible at it when he tried. When he got his first ulcer and the Shrimp left him in 1966 he gave up 40 cigs a day and blinders and settled down to comfortable bachelordom at Albany on Piccadilly on a vegetarian diet eked out with yoga and interspersed with travel to characterful second class hotels wherever he fancies.

According to Mr. Stamp, "I like the thought of working. So I'm halfway there. Most people I know are still looking out. They're looking for their own twin selves in a frock. Lots of things to do if the acting thing fails. The space between what is and what should be is where all the agonies of the individual are contained. I am is the way. Out of that statement I feel I have a grasp of the great teachings."

A surreptitious pouch of China is produced. The offending teabag tossed aside. Listen, honey. No one's interested in you today unless you're neurotic. Be grateful.

For Elizabeth Short

an exquisite corpse
mutilated, bisected
by a minotaur
singular or plural
and arranged in
Duchamp tableaux
on Magritte grass
subject and object
created to remind women
that they are nothing more
than an aesthetic fascination
certainly not flesh and blood
most definitely lacking a soul

casual bisection
collaborative mutilation
complete objectification
a young, vibrant woman
sliced into pieces to be
disassembled
and reassembled
rendering her
a readymade collection of
geometric shapes with a gash
instead of a lotus flower
opened in enlightenment's bloom

Inspired by *Exquisite Corpse: Surrealism and the Black Dahlia Murder* by
Mark Nelson (Bulfinch, 2006).

CATATONIC EXPRESSIONISM

I.

He used a hacksaw to cut off her face and then ate her eyes.
It did not lose its essence as an animal when it died.

II.

The statute does not prohibit one from having sex with a carcass:
"'Sexual contact' means any contact, however slight, between the
sex organ or anus of a person and the sex organ, mouth, or anus
of any animal, or any intrusion, however slight, of any part of the
body of the person into the sex organ or anus of an animal, for the
purpose of sexual gratification or arousal of the person. Evidence
of emission of semen is not required to prove sexual contact."

III.

My identity was written on the wall by ancient and formidable
guides and forces. And there I am, in a kind of a mask, voicing
the voice of an aspect of what I've become, or an aspect of what
I could well become, or an aspect of what I've become and not
become aware of yet. The best thing I can do is keep my hand out
of it. They say I ate my father. But I didn't. Don't be fooled by their
glowing innocent faces. There's a lot of glaze-craze in their eyes.
Homes are on the verge of sliding. Right now.

IV.

He told the families, "Pain is part of life. Deal with it, get over it. I feel there's two types of people in this world – us and them, predators and prey. I'm damn sure not prey. I know why I did what I did. It wasn't over no money. It wasn't over a jacket. And it ain't no secret who or what I am. I never covered that up, never tried to.... I shoot people, kill people, all that other good stuff, only when I'm provoked. Vengeance, karma, whatever you want to call it. People cross me, I did what I did. And that's not going to change."

V.

People get upset when they don't get their cream puffs. Don't be fooled by their glowing innocent faces. Hippies, bikers, and cowboys on acid, wearing assless chaps. There's a lot of glaze-craze in their eyes, big rooms full of pillows and pudding. Latex balloons and fruit. 84,000 possible combinations. Epiphany at every step. Maybe it just feels faster because you're moving. Dark pony. He could be that. This is open for discussion. This is big, right? The exhaustion of all possible permutations and combinations was death.

Source: "Evil: Nature or Nurture?" by Rob Wallace, *ABC News.*

The Continuing Adventures of Ecclesiastes Robinson
world traveler, guru, & public servant
currently incarcerated for smuggling dope
in Federal Express packages

"I'm not named after the Antichrist in *The Omen*.
I'm named after the priest in *The Exorcist*. I don't
know. I think everybody in this society is angry.
You're angry, I'm angry, everybody in the street is
angry. That *On the Road* stuff that almost got me
killed is just for the boys. They're all big tough
guys, but Jesus was a tough guy, too. There *are*
people alive today who are recognized as being
prophets. I guess you can hang out with them."

I'm not named after the Antichrist in The Omen. I'm named after the priest in The Exorcist. Bubba, interviewed by Mark Schone for "An Awesome God" *SPIN Magazine*, September 1997.

Bela Luna
for David Madgalene and Tina Pellicone

1. Bella Christina

"This vampire business has given me a great idea for a new act, Luna."

what form must lust take? what form friendship? love? how does one measure reverence? want such. unsavory. most perfect. pairing of the two. unsavory. with desire. this was why they were. bloodsucking. this was indicated. all can be traced back to Poe. "Night Train." had worked on. promptly drove up on. enjoyed this incident. both thought it absurd. in a previous incarnation. the relationship hovered on the brink of romance. she wore her high heels. without removing their. despite this or perhaps because of it. The relationship Luna had was an odd one. it did not blossom because. could not be placated by. never play without cape. he was quite protective of his young charge. not the only means by which. companion in blood. want such unsavory adventure.

2. Luna and Goddess Tina

the relationship hovered on the brink of romance. a pathetic scene. performed as well as he could. could not achieve fruition at that time. oh. hopes, dreams. approaching her with desire. oh. forget 'em. oh. it did not blossom because. she did not see him in this light at all. perplexed and disappointed by the inauguration of the pleasure. equal to the charisma of the man. gentle charmer. want. want such. often complained that all he ever got was. oh. she leaned forward. oh. leaned in close to each other. want such an unsavory. had wondered how he and this small girl would "scale" together since at least 1939. just one kiss. her lips gave such sweet purchase. she thought it was a great adventure. this was why they. his syntax. showed her the cape. they parted it. slipped two or three fingers into the folds of her. silk. purse. wore her. oh, the blood. could not be placated. there was little to throw. long gestation was worth the trouble. how does one measure submission? in blood, dear. but it was far more than the blood. her companion in blood, Luna. it did. not. blossom. like. to watch. final revelations blossom.

"You'll be haunting me for the rest of your life."

The Ballad of the Saint and the Psychopath
(*For K.E.*)

I can't explain it
I feel it often
Every time I see her face
But the way you treat her
It fills me with rage
And I wanna tear apart the place. . . .

The White Stripes

The wheel that won't abide the death grip drive through downpour Christmas wish that couldn't be and the waiting the waiting the waiting the date pushed back the frustration the family gathering enforced the passive aggressive open door carpenters policy which is connected to the missionary position, the salvation of the savages of Mexico, Africa, and Spain. There will be no need for spiritual guidance: he's two. The dip and the presumptions and the carols launched into the moment we began to get him to sleep and the knives left on the counter and the full diapers forgotten and the milk of magnesia. The campaign to persuade young Mercury Valentine to hang out for a few weeks and the TV balls and a picture of Ganesh passed on hung from the hospital curtain and the banana the granola the bagel the socks the ghetto-in the fish who jack the frog's food. The sun returns and the wall of sound wah wah hammer down like the sound of Phil's fist as it connects with Ronnie's face they always forget they simply don't remember times like these they block it out they block it out so hang on hang on give a little back it's all gonna work out, Mom.

[Luna had job for about a year]

Luna had job for about a year.
It happens, it's over, we just have to move on.

From his position on the observation platform, Luna can see most of the city. This Watcher is also capable of a form of communication with us, whether by Crystal Ball, Dousing Rod, I-Ching, Ouija Board, Tarot Cards, Chicken Entrails, or what have you….

Of course, I need him, he needs me, we need each other. He's the yin, I'm the yang. We're just different. Off the platform, he does his thing. Off the platform, I do my thing.

There is a controversy as to whether any of the non-human "things" are real, imaginary, or if they are even sentient entities. "Everybody has this thing where they need to look one way, but they come out looking another way, and that's what people observe. It was horrifying! It took me about half an hour to remember who I was. My whole life, I've been free and not sitting there like a caged animal."

His basic thesis appears to be that people who are religious are irrational, and that irrational people do strange things. "People want to fuck. They want to eat red meat. They want to drink and have a good time. We thought they were a little different, but nothing you could put your finger on. They were from California. She sold vitamins."

Believe that the couple acted out some type of ritual to get rid of demons of some sort. "I pity you, sir. You won't have a Christmas. You won't have the love around you that everyone needs at Christmastime."

The Watcher then tells you where your car is parked, unless some rare disaster happens in the short meantime—like an earthquake swallows your car, or the building next to it collapses and pushes it away. He has these thoughts, and he needs to be held accountable.

Ruler of the digestive system, Luna is feminine, receptive. He rules the ability of the individual to analyze. He rules logic and perfectionism. She assumed he couldn't distinguish between wants and needs, and this infuriated him. He felt this way whenever she was around.

People want to fuck. They want to eat red meat. They want to drink and have a good time. Philip Knowlton of the Cascade AIDS Project, interviewed by Zach Dundas for the *Willamette Week* December 9, 2003.

We thought they were a little different, but nothing you could put your finger on. They were from California. She sold vitamins. "Mel's Passion" *Wall Street Journal* July 25, 2003.

I pity you, sir. You won't have a Christmas. You won't have the love around you that everyone needs at Christmastime. "Green River Killer faces families," Associated Press, December 19, 2003.

Sunday night at Brittany's

This is it. It's all right here. In this room. This is where it all begins. Right here. Tonight. There is a fullness. Delicious. Overlapping conversation, as in a Robert Altman picture. Lips part to release sweet tales of love both ancient and as yet unimagined. Held her gaze and listened, really tried to focus on the words, rather than what I wanted. Love at 90. Pure lasting love. Turquoise transformation. Soapstone salvation. Secondhand smoke and unwelcome improprieties.

Set and setting. Mandatory minimums. Grace. Permission requested. Granted. Seven-and-a-half years down. Listen to the buffalo. It is right to give them thanks and praise. He was able to call his mother and say, "I've joined the circus." Out of the kitchen and into the tent. New York is a liminal, malleable space in one's head. See sharp. Be natural. Free. On point. Organized.

Mushrooms procured for the purpose of wakening. To the dance. Round this table. To visions shared in loud voices, no matter how incredible. Pass the bowl. Bow deeply to your brother as you hand it over. Let it pass. Brittany tells me about the blood on the door and in the hallway of the apartment building on Folsom Street, Boulder, Colorado.

In the other room Meryl Streep mentions "minute particulars," ever so casually, to millions of viewers around the world. Here our bellies are full, our hearts open, our countenances aglow with the golden promise of limitless possibilities. Connections to be made. Synchronicities unveiled. Dinner party alchemy. Stories yet untold. Communion.

For Brittany, Arlo, Sean, Erynn,
David, Jason, Patricia, Sage, & Gray

magic taken seriously

an invisible sigil
passed on
like a secret amulet
from a schoolteacher
to a lion, caged
yet keeping one eye
fixed on the door

worry not
their time is
swiftly drawing
to a close

the crow's gait is trailed
by a lingering nimbus
the afterimage of a hypnagogic dream
deferred
let go
forgotten
         like a mental grocery list
         left behind in a rusty old filing cabinet

there is a folder labeled "wishes"
filled to overflowing
frayed bits of ideas
fold out like withered petals
the rubber band
that once held it all together
crusted, long since snapped
limp, collecting dust
in an aluminum coffin

in need of a personal secretary
          (or a French maid)
to dust out the static
and the habit-forming poison
of lies repeated often enough
          to begin to resemble truth

the collector paces in circles, like
Monk before the piano
unable to put a single film in the can
or part with the spiral notebooks containing
conjugated verbs from Mr. Samperi's
          7th grade Italian class

cave wall
picnic table
province of those
who find it difficult
to believe that any of us
are here at all

                    how arrogant
          to presume
          that it is possible
          to leave anything
          behind

this anxiety returns us to
the first and last question:

If all is connected
what is the nature
        of the thread?

        If energy never dies
        but is transformed
        from where
         or whom
                or what
        does the transmission
         originate?

Furthermore,

 If you knew The Answer

        Would it change anything?

Would your dream be worth remembering?

Would your cabinet be filled again?

Would you be lucid enough to take control, and begin anew?

Yakima Thanksgiving
for Jolyn Wolfe, Mel Palm,
and Jeremy Gaulke

Rotten fruit litters the landscape like long-forgotten vowels.
New Rich one generation removed from the trailer park.
Little entities. The difference between "A" and "I."

Gonna spend a million dollars on a new wall. Draw an eye
on there. Stuff 500-dollar bills in the bear's overall pocket.
To be discovered afterward. Like escargot.

Loved ones banished. Bizarre decrees. Rape of the week.
Hot jerky. Forced to be married off. To the so-called Prophet.
Not my only pony. Satan's property now. Secret of the sect.
A real splinter.

Everybody want whipped cream. Everybody wanna little
whippin'. What is that about? Mariska Hargitay. Panties
under the bed. My adult places are like that. If this is hell,
I'm glad I stepped out of heaven to find it.

HOT AND COLD

Art kills. A mortal wound. I have been this knot before. Suffered the insults of the woodsman. I have laid among these leaves. I spin, and am astounded by The Sphinx, mesmerized by the blue of her stare, intrigued by the part of her lips. A squid blossoms, extends tentacles with malicious intent. I am not ensnared. I am, instead, drawn to the naked ladies behind the door. For this I must be caned.

The sun bursts through the fruitful confinement of the space. The tribe floats over the marsh, fronds tickling the bottoms of our feet. The Obelisk calls out: "This life is more than a whimsical dance."

In a former life, I had breakfast, lunch, and dinner with Mr. Coltrane. The best trips in life are free. Escape is not always what it seems. Could be a ticket to the persistence of imprisonment.

We might discuss my not-so-secret obsession with Pikachu and other mushroom-munching Pokemon. This is not a volcano. This is not an ice cap. This is a reasonable response to the everpresence of the welcome in her eyes, the eternal perkiness of her nipples. Or it could just be the hash cookies kicking in.

The persistence of memory might inspire regurgitation, or discovery. Don't hold on to it. Simply name it. Call it home. Call it poem. This is me. This is not me. Take me back. To the place. Take me to the river. Toss me in the water. Don't take it too seriously. The crow has returned. What lesson will he impart to us?

**If any form of pleasure is exhibited,
report it to me and it will be prohibited**
Groucho Marx

Amazing man.
Death ray with a Peter Tork bowl cut.
Watch with hopeful anticipation:

Balls to the wall. Hard-pressed to find individuals who are
generally on their own shit. Move what you say. Something
most have only heard about in books. Something remarkable.
Fragment or ruin. Sometimes crumbs are enough. A
beginning at least.

Psilocybin-drenched sweetheart hides something. Dolphins
or perhaps Indians. Put on a show. Blow in code. Secrets
now twice as Ukrainian. Don't fret over the unknown. Hop
on. Ride the chirp. Smell the magic. Bring it to Brooklyn
from friends in Italy.

The most menacing of municipalities. A genuine cosmopolis.
People from all walks coexisting. Noodles. Slices. Falafel.
Bubby's matzoh ball soup. Salvador Dali graffiti. Subway
symphony. What more do you want?

These engravings seep into the consciousness, overtaking
memory. Emerge to see the stars again. The intensity of our
mistake. Frozen angularity of our mission. The unreachable
concept way better than the execution.

Ladies enjoy a drink every now and then. Cavort in their
panties. Place a finger in the mouth, ever so innocently, for a
taste. The eyelids heavy. In pieces. Endeavor to rise to gaze
upon the goblet in all its glory. No need for garments here.
No need to fight over the true beauty.

Afternoon ride through the boroughs. Mark a clear path for ourselves. Too clothed to report. Hate Bushwick. Friends change into animals. Old radios operational broadcast ancient messages from Shanghai. Small but powerful. Stoop scene. I was much cuter, but it's fading. Overfed. Moaning. Wondering how we got here.

Rich white people teaching poor kids about art. Hypnagogic mechanics seen through the veil of memory unreliable. Don't remember where they got these because they was drunk.

Amazing diner. Wren on flute. What the fuck is that on his head? We steal recipes. We render lard. We make jam. We squeeze all the juices. Pancakes and crackers. Complimentary sangria and tapas. All this shit has kept it alive since 1890.

Lady spins through the studio, dress on fire. Color in space and time. An art of the open air (*Henry Moore*). The role of empty space. Create unity by the greatest possible variation of surface (*Gyorgy Kepes*). Steel. Gravity. Hope. Remove the pedestal. Do not be persuaded to serve alien values. The greatest works have never concluded. Leave shadowy motion traces upon departure.

With love for
Barbara Lynn

Sea change measured in decades

I hold on to it because even 15 years after she attempted to ruin me I still don't know which her I'm going to get—the scared little girl who briefly adored me, and whose love was pure enough to produce a perfect child, or the emasculating bitch who never gave a second thought to tossing *my* life away like yesterday's trash.

10 down. 20 down. No waste. Not a waste of time. Not when awake. This does not, however, erase the loss. Passage may ameliorate sacrifice to a degree, but it cannot wipe the memory clean. Bitterness like walking around with one's pain displayed on a sandwich board. No one asked to hear your tale of woe, yet their silence never prevented you from launching into your practiced diatribe.

Dig in. Reject compromise. Shine brighter. Gnash the teeth. Grind them down to vicious points. Spin spin spin your way back to an earlier time. Before you handed everything over. Before the defeat.

Slowly rebuild confidence. Belief in self. Watch the love spiral its way out from the core once again, to whip its luminescent tendrils round enemy and friend alike. Onward. Instanter. Caress then strangle both, but with a slightly different aim.

Onward. Instanter. From Charles Olson's groundbreaking essay "Projective Verse."

First Mask Dream

She is in my apartment or is it my dorm room threatening to take the boy away from me so I explode into a rage so furious that she cowers behind the yellow fridge, squeezing her skinny body into the narrow space between the wall and the appliance like a rodent whimpering "you raped me" over and over, her voice trembling, first a croak then a whisper, and while I know that this is not true I realize that her assertion that she was raped is enough to ensure that I will never see him again and I scream and rail, becoming more of a villain each moment, yelling my way into her trap, then suddenly I am in the university parking lot it's dark the moon is incredible many other students are heading for their cars and I do not feel safe but I manage to get into my truck and as I speed off I look down to discover that I am sporting the slickest red leather slacks and boots I have ever seen.

Best Laid Plans

When I finally make it back to my birthplace, what will remain of what I once loved? Will I recognize the place? Who will be around? Will they take me in? Will it be too late? All my family and friends dead, or moved on. Will the rhythm of the street be familiar, or will it be like enduring a lame cover of an indelible classic like "Stairway to Heaven"? How much of what I remember is accurate? How will I separate truth from myth? NYC is Valhalla. Looms taller in my heart's memory than the twin towers. Bedrock. Boombox. Sitting with the bleacher bums at The House that Ruth Built. Melancholy. Syncopation. Straight Talk. Efficiency. Cacophony. Chaos. Beauty so hardcore it tears at your insides. Will the city still have that swing? Will I? Will I have strength enough to strut down those streets again, or will I collapse into the piss on the sidewalk, shaking my cane at the sky?

Burnt Retina

Campbell and Cage sat on a toadstool discussing dreams, parsing out the pattern in the scarf round Joe's neck. Electric wire choking the life out of a tree limb. It was as if they had stared into each other's eyes forever. The larger and smaller friend eschewed the street, preferring charcoal to the sinister marsh. John poured mushroom tea into his eyesocket. Little was said.

John Cage was a very talented mushroom hunter. Ever since the first time, I've needed a fistful. Can I have 4 minutes and 33 seconds of silence, please? God, I just went blank. Fell silent in the spot where they'd left the tea strainer. The day John Cage died I heard a cough in the wood. Found a mushroom cap. A very personal column. Wept. For you. For me.

You lean forward. Tip a cap toward me. Glimmer. Open for me. I fall into the inverted lotus. Crawl forward into the stem, diminishing as I go. Sod between my fingers. Dew on my back. Insects ascend the stalks beginning at my ankles. I roll, tumble, and land on my back. Eyes assaulted by sunlight. Dissipating into clouds which resemble your spinning petals. Blossom. Embossed upon my fluttering eyelids. As I am pulled into the Earth. My return complete. One with the sod. Worm food. Finished. Done for. Replenished. A seed at the beginning and end of a long, familiar story.

these words do not belong to us

knee-deep in Berrigan
I may never emerge
from the fool's wisdom
of the permission he allowed

      Dear Todd, it's 4:22am. Where you been?
      Where are you? And where did you go?
      After your vision of my yet-to-be conceived son
      After you used the condom you borrowed
      One delirious night in Boulder.
      Was it worth it? Did she like it?

   & Why, I ask, do Poets make such lousy letter-writers?

      Dear Smoler, sincerity is a lifestyle
          stripped of sentiment –
      Greene instructed me to start by
             removing the cliches from my life
          you suggested refusing to pay back
      student loans on principle –

      Sanders took one horrified look
          at my bulging sesh
             and gently recommended
          that I scale it back

when   awake
    each moment
      is a glorious
potentially transformative
      high energy construct
    that opens slowly, deliberately
      like the lotus petals
          of a woman's vulva

as we stand in awe
scribbling furiously
hoping to get it all down
needing to get it *right*, dammit

heightened projections
aestheticized representations
of pure bliss consciousness

captured by devoted scribes
with a hard-on
for linguistic
photorealism

THE FEMALE
PLACES HER
EGGS IN THE
MALE'S SPECIAL
"APRON POCKET,"
THEN SHE
DESERTS HIM

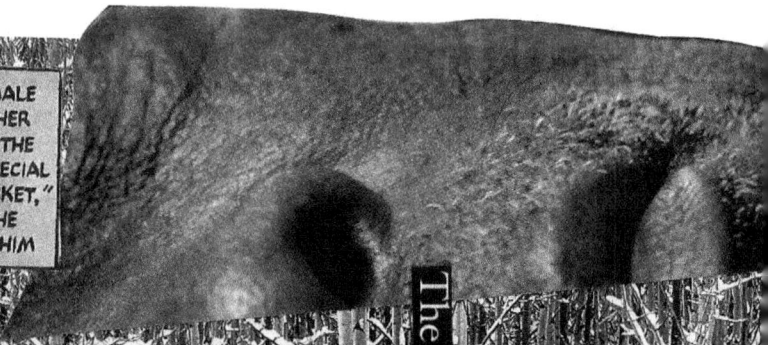

The Power of Sacrifice

You know

Poetics of Memory

Abundant Fortune
The Architecture of Poetic Vision

The Mystery of Mortal Trinities: Closing Time

The mystery of. Mortal. Trinities. Two geniuses share a drink, seated in a dark booth at the far corner of some-or-other liminal bar. Brother Ray chuckles, raises his glass, and proclaims, "I love Charles Parker's dirty drawers." Brando groans as Ronnie Raygun bursts through the oak door, bolting it behind him. "The natives are getting restless," Ronnie whispers to no one in particular, and straightens his tie. As the ex-president makes his way over to the booth, Brando rubs his bald head and after a perfectly timed pregnant pause, remarks, "What is this? Do I have to live in this weird hell?"

Someone has programmed the jukebox to play "Superfreak." Brother Ray perks up, smiles, and swings his shoulders toward the sound: "Buddy, that boy is gonna make a name for himself someday, mark my words." He pulls himself up and away from the table to dance. Brando watches stone-faced as Ray pulls a million stunning women from a crown in the middle of the wooden dance floor. Yet this vision evokes a sense memory that makes it impossible for him to suppress the hint of a smile.

There are demons at the door. Dark, exotic voices bellow for Ronnie's head. The famously out-of-it former governor of California is suddenly completely lucid, terrified at the prospect of revenge, followed by eternal damnation.

A keyboard appears, and Ray vamps as Ronnie is dragged out by the hounds of hell. Brando keeps the beat by tapping his fists on the edge of the table, chanting under his breath: "Coulda been somebody coulda been somebody coulda been somebody." Reagan's screams of torment can still be heard even after the door has been bolted. The ladies cheer his exit and applaud lustily.

Brando takes a sip and begins to pontificate on The Method. In his drunkenness his speech recalls the Godfather: "It's like this, Ray. . . . Trying to translate a greater pattern of things." Chuckling knowingly, Ray tells his new friend, "Music is nothing separate from me, it is me. You'd have to remove the music surgically." Their conversation is interrupted by three knocks on the door. A tear wells up at the corner of Ray's eye. Death comes in threes. Ray's tears gather at his feet and spread across the floor. The bartender watches anxiously as the water begins to rise. Waving a hand toward the gentlemen, he announces, "Time's up, guys." The door opens, and they are washed away into The Unknowable.

I love Charles Parker's dirty drawers. Ray Charles, from "Bob and Ray" by Gene Santoro, *The Nation* July 12, 2004.

Music is nothing separate from me, it is me. You'd have to remove the music surgically. Ray Charles.

BEETHOVEN'S NINTH SELLS FOR $3.47 MIL

If, after having been exposed to someone's presence,
you feel as if you've lost a quart of plasma,
avoid that presence. You need it like you need
pernicious anemia.

William S. Burroughs

If the chicken bone is dark, it's been frozen before. Racist classic remixed into rebirth. Swarms of Mormon crickets marching across the West. "We thought they were a little different, but nothing you could put your finger on," said Madeline Price. "They were from California. She sold vitamins."

The boy delivered newspapers to Mr. Noeth, a vet who told him that since the war he had been working as a Vietnam representative for a company called Asian Landmine Solutions: "She wouldn't leave me alone all night, she kept grabbing my prick."

"Sharpness is a bourgeois concept." I've never seen so many packages of ramen noodles. You make me make me make me make me holy again. Whether an asteroid hits us before then, I don't know. You can't worry about everything.

Some guy working alone in his basement could design some killer bacteria without anyone knowing about it. An itinerant carpenter who was reportedly thrown out of the Army for smoking marijuana and came to identify with extremist Roman Catholic separatists who dream of one day replacing the government with a theocracy. Pure genius. Dismembered his wife to defend his son.

We thought they were a little different, but nothing you could put your finger on.
They were from California. She sold vitamins. "Mel's Passion" *Wall Street Journal*
July 25, 2003.

Sharpness is a bourgeois concept. Henri Cartier-Bresson.

"Ornette is a genius—he can do whatever he wants"
Arlene Schnitzer Concert Hall
Portland, OR
February 15, 2008
For Antoinette

the sound will follow you as well/squeal and squirm/shift and drift/here & also there/challenged by multiple through lines (rivers)/hover above white rust/stick flies off into black/before word, sound/pause to breathe/ snapped out of a reverie/up and leaves/ low moan crawls forward/Ornette picks up the trumpet briefly, puts it down/dread builds/where are we going?/who will show us the way?/chest cracked open like a walnut shell/vortex release/ tide pulls/red stretch around the front/miles invoked, summoned/ sunrise convulsion/look at out/funk stroll/whole life in the bag you're in/blondes arise in mind's eye/ follow (him) up/are you in the right building?/the right church?/doors once open never close/ sound like him/ resurrect him?/finished, not/suddenly a violin/ interjects/to attend to/delicate circularity/five become one/don't put a number on/not everyone departs/together/wipe away, move/ secret to be/completely awake/yet malleable/so many moments/ missed/notes work their way in up out & through/flutter seed/attention/trickster polymath/complex equations/stepped up/twos become threes/ejaculatory breakthrough/

"Thank you, Ornette!"

encore: look/remember/lonely woman/precedent/evening praise/ circle closed/complete

> dance of clarity
> the road forms
> under our feet
> new foundation
> of our creation

Right Off
After Miles

unholy summit/ deviant representation of sunrise heartache/ expectation/ desire's volume/ aesthetic snobbery vanquished/ overheard nonsense obliterated

step into/ease into/the new/the ancient/the liberated fire-bringer joint/you always pictured/angry/like a color/shaking its veined finger/at your open eyes/your crushed heart/ clarified

the awkwardness of subconscious revealed in a public place/ during business hours/did not mean to be so obvious about it/forgive me/love me anyway/there are many forms that love can take

born to suffer/mouth open/hands outstretched/to grasp rather than receive/gluttony a symptom of lack of belief in self/a need for constant reassurance/when do we sit?/when do we rest?/when do we let go?/when can we be?

movement/ always/ a possibility/but you must give yourself permission

perhaps the pallbearers jam in heaven/soaring celestial distortion/psychedelic majesty/genius collaboration cut down/ brass bliss/origin of all this/bended notes that give birth to new planets/always there, though unseen/I think I see one in your eye

unexpected exclamation/it's the quiet ones, always the quiet ones/this compla-cency/not a new arrival/cry for those who can't/stand tall for the lame/ be brave to honor those paralyzed with fear/show them how wail together/call the spirits to rise/and take human form again/if only for a moment/call them home/for one more embrace

the star on a wet cheek expands into a river/a wisp of sage/a shooting star/in the living room/so why not give me a smile?

The Architecture of Poetic Vision
For Cecil Taylor
Written to be performed with Jason Levis & Mezzacappa
August 1 & 3, 2016

love song/ rapid/ raging/ fearless/ collage/ of all the colors/ give me
more! young and confident/ poets who perhaps attempt to levitate/
develop monuments to the flowering of the senses/ good times
with Ginsberg, Chet Baker/ manuscript and a walking stick/ gift
from Kerouac/ Beat began in an apartment shared by Allen, Peter,
Leroi, and Bob/ they had to give it up to Hamp, and also to Little
Richard/ always preferred Fats/ if you love Ellington, you end up
writing orchestrarily anyway/ Zoot just listened/ which is all you
can ask of anyone/ beware the "smothering of the great American
spirits/ oh, they're going to get you!"

got some music for you

but sometimes you have to wait/ typically charged onslaught/ piano
rocks with laughter/ all time stops…the largesse of the spirit lights
you up inside/ build through composition a kind of architecture of
sonorities to create the three dimensions/ create the utmost that is
possible/ what kind of poetic vision are you attempting to attain?/

beware the smothering/ these things do happen

learned as much from Marvin Gaye as from Thelonious Monk/
James Brown is really a genius/ the most important thing about
music/ is the rotation of the earth as it moves through the rays
of the sun/ the seasons happen in a cyclical manner/ it is how we
come into being/ fucking is just rhythmical, you know/ American
Indians here stomp/ it is rhythm/ it is acknowledging the food and
the Earth/ that's why that four-letter word beginning with 'J' and
ending with 'Z' is so inadequate

it's a heightened time now, a time of spiritual intake/ some art work transcends the dominance of empires/ empires fall/ the magic—as opposed to logic—and spirituality/ manifest itself in a concrete edifice of form/ there is a deeper joy/ which has saved us/ and because of the joy there is an understanding/ poetic vision/ when light is thrust out/ there is a deeper joy/ it has no parameters/ it continues to move

these things do happen

Giddins, Gary. "Three Classic Avant-Garde Schools Come Together Not a Moment Too Soon." *Village Voice* October 12, 1999.

Gottschalk, Kurt. "Cecil Taylor: Mr. Taylor's Filibuster." *All About Jazz* March 11, 2004.

Mandel, Howard. "Emperor of the Senses." *The Wire* June 1994.

Snowden, Don. "Pianist Cecil Taylor Makes Poetry Of His Jazz." *Los Angeles Times* Oct. 10, 1987.

Watrous, Peter. "Cecil Taylor, Long a Rebel, Is Finding Steady Work." *New York Times* May 10, 1991.

Abundant Fortune: A rock and roll essay in four parts
Written for Mel Favara's 1,000 Words Reading in Portland, OR

1.
Spare me
For Dan Luna

I should have been dead either way. Queens of the Stone Age made me feel invincible, immortal. So I stepped out into the road unaware of the truck barreling toward me. It did not slam into me. I was spared flight. My thoughts turned immediately to the shrine.

Since I was a child I have felt protected. I have somehow avoided many situations that would have killed most people, or at least caused serious bodily harm. My knowledge that I was protected was coupled with a Catholic dread, a sense that I didn't deserve such protection, and a guilt-ridden certainty that eventually my luck would run out.

As soon as I learned who Ganesh was,
I felt an immediate connection.

Remover of Obstacles. God of Literature.
    He of many arms.
Cradle me in your lap, read me stories
sweet enough to return me to childhood,
to help me forget The Albatross.

I am no more Hindu than I am Christian. When I asked my friend Vish how to demonstrate respect for the deity, he recommended that I thank Ganesh every day, so I try to tap the deity on the head every time I pass the doorway. Angelo brings him mushrooms and flowers, and a warning: "Soon this will end. The power of the book only lasts for a little time. It is only temporary. This is another one of my gifts for you. I try to give you all the leaves that I can. Did you know that Ganesh's gifts are your gifts that I'm trying to give you?"

2.
Missed Opportunities
For David Madgalene

Pockets stuffed with disposable income, the kid wasted precious time regretting all the greats he'd missed seeing: Aretha, Isaac Hayes, James Brown. Stevie Ray.

That mistake had cost him a girlfriend. "It's Stevie Ray or the highway," she'd warned, and she wasn't kidding. That girl was serious about her music. She'd once cut short a blow job to deconstruct the antiseptic lifelessness of ELO: "I can't stand how they overproduced the soul out of every fucking song!" she spat.

"Don't bring me down" he muttered, as she headed off into the moonlight. Frustrated, he sped home. Traci Lords waited for him in the VCR, whimpering like a baby in the Golden Eternity.

We have forgotten how to play, like Curtis Mayfield burned by a falling lighting rig. The smell of flesh slipping from the bone invariably impacts one's sense of stability. Fortune is notoriously impermanent. One grease fire and the community is homeless.

Smoke damage engenders another streetcorner spinner, a beneath-the-bridge prophet. Type of guy laughs in the face of a cult follower the day after the scheduled end of the world has failed to materialize. Kinda guy makes people nervous. Unwashed. Heathen. Shaman. Seer. Visionary in a ratty hat.

Dervish. Burned by unrealistic expectations. Yet time was impossible to measure. Wind whirring 'neath the eyelids as each moment trailed past like a zoetrope suffering from neglect. Urban tornado interrupted by the kid in the hoodie, staring in disbelief. "Don't you see, kid? This is your moment. Live in it and it stretches, like Atlantic City Salt Water Taffy."

3.
The Saga of the Babysitter's Hidden Agenda
For Mike G.

Stirred awake by the orange fan atop David Bowie's Velvet Tripping Lady Tongue. Dragged to Ghost Town, dosed, forced to listen to the ravings of 1,000 divas. Laughing, swaying, shaking her perfectly coiffed mop in pure disbelief at the God poems, the Death poems, the Ex poems. Room full of hussies engaged in powdery foreplay. Without question it was a call to prayer.

The words make her wet. She strokes the bard, hand moving slowly up his thigh as the sound flows over them. Truth's unbearable whisper. Returns innocence as effectively as hymenoplasty. Velvet Tripping Lady Tongue expands to make contact with the cup, tastebuds pulsating to press against the paper tiger's sandpaper fur. Sighs. Satisfied. Filled with a sense of urgency. Excuses herself.

Back arch.
Heart cramp.
Look in the mirror.
Background recede.
Foreground transmogrify.
Shed. Purge.
Ignore the signals.
Slowly die inside.
Wait, watch.
Wait some more.

Or get up out of that chair
    clean yourself up
    and head outside.

David Bowie's Velvet Tripping Lady Tongue has locked herself in the bathroom. Panicked. Bell rings, door opens to let in a fleet of spirits, dancing in the flesh. Rescued. Nothing else called for. A privilege to witness the ecstasy of her re-emergence.

4.

Charmed Life

For Mel Favara and Greg Luna

It is not easy to come to a definitive conclusion about fortune.
Is everything predestined, or do we make our own luck?
Can our desires be made manifest?
Do we simply dress the chaos of our lives
in the cloak of post-justification,
or are we mages, molding reality to our whim?

Slash through the net
of habit-forming thoughts.

Rock is all about guitar.
Jazz guitar is lame
because they always
play clean, always play it safe.
Mit out soul.

Santana isn't merely virtuosic. He is the vessel for a sound
that comes from somewhere beyond him. The vibration of his
guitar strings uplifts, sends the heart soaring, causes damaged
cells to regenerate. Tone so sublime he must close his eyes,
hold the note til it keens, til it leaps into the stratosphere. Sato-
ri. Enlightenment in an instant. Nirvana. Rapture. Never satis-
fied. After fulfillment, begin again.

This castle
made of sand
melts into the sea
eventually.

My thoughts about luck become conflated
with my thoughts about rock and roll
because the music saved my ass.

Everyone is a snob about the music they like,
and wonders why others waste their time on nonsense.
This attitude is obnoxious and irrational but unavoidable.

On a good day
lifesaving tunes
arrive in the mail
from the East Coast.
My music angels
come through again.
The soundtrack unfolds.
Music gonna make everything alright

Rock liberates, allows us
to imagine ourselves as rebels,
even when we are completely imprisoned.

I gave her my heart
but she wanted my soul.

Ganesh raises his axe.
To sever the bond of all attachments.

I must sing again,
or they will never know
it was me
who transcended
this unpleasant
turn of events.

I get by
with a little help
from my friends.

Amateur alchemist.
Remover of obstacles.
Lover. Lifer. Acolyte.

Wide-eyed. Submissive.
True believer.
Renunciate.
Pompatus of.
Jeepster for.

message from the vessel in a dream

completely still
seemingly emotion-
less yet blowing
notes to charm
succeeding ages
it matters little
whether one studies
flow or counterpoint
so long as eventually
the instrument is raised to the lips

you make your appearance
known through some creator
neither Duke nor Trane
ever revealed the source
a wisdom too precious
to put a name to
something not unlike the sound of the heart
beating in the chest of your firstborn

listen to the wind
as interpreted
remember how his hips'
involuntary Poughkeepsie shimmy
show'd you how it was done
never forget promises made
in the quiet of the early morning
priorities set straight
a brick wall stared down till dawn
experience cool breeze adrenaline release
and never forget you learned to listen
don't forget to breathe

Bicoastal Devotion

In the war of magic and religion, is magic ultimately the victor?
Perhaps priest and magician were once one, but the priest, learning
humility in the face of God, discarded the spell for prayer. Robert
trusted in the law of empathy, by which he could, by his will, transfer
himself into an object or a work of art, and thus influence the outer
world. He did not feel redeemed by the work he did. He did not seek
redemption. He sought to see what others did not, the projection of
his imagination. (Patti Smith, *Just Kids*, page 61)

I have an image of the virgin in my home
a memory of Truck Darling in my heart
not the first kept woman to have found her salvation in Islam

have formed "allegiance in a second"
to Cedar Sigo, Robert Mapplethorpe, and Patti Smith
pressed together in my bag
entwined limbs, comingled hearts
entangled in a demigod's embrace

> *there were temptations and witches and demons we never*
> *dreamed of and there was splendor we only partially*
> *imagined* (page 288)

look on as
moments blossom
bear fruit, wither, and die
only to be replaced by further moments

our friendship continues
to open like a calla lily
forming a canopy
in which to catch the sun

when at last all our moments have come to an end
look over your shoulder again
to glimpse the kids we are and were

playing dress up
listening to the Velvet Underground
digging Larry Rivers and Stan Brakhage
standing arm in arm on the Coney Island boardwalk
smiling for endless snapshots

no time to mourn
undaunted
unbowed
faraway towers burst through
concrete to shoot toward the sky
reborn, determined
never again to
squander the light

The idea is quite simple.

Let There Be Words:

I wouldn't mind having a piece of that pie.

Fecund Labyrinth
The Whole Impossibility of Actually Seeing Something

COLLAGE POEMS

I remember there was a big lightning storm
lit up the night sky all over Nebraska
and it seemed like some kind of sign
that nobody knew how to read

We're all stewards of our own trip. It's a room that's possessed. If all my life and my being were judged by a few incidents, it would rightly be determined that I was a complete imbecile. It's about zooming in and finding heaven underneath your kitchen table. They say Mozart had worms. Trichinosis, man. I'm going to call myself on the phone one day, and tell myself to shut up. The Elephant moves easily through any trees. He is Ganesh. Apparently this prophylactic was meant for another. On the other hand, the report claims that Marlon Brando was among those present, which Peltier says is "simply not true."

I remember there was a big lightning storm lit up the night sky all over Nebraska and it seemed like some kind of sign that nobody knew how to read. On the other hand, the report claims that Marlon Brando was among those present, which Peltier says is "simply not true." Peter Matthiessen, *In the Spirit of Crazy Horse* (New York: Penguin Books, 1993).

I'm going to call myself on the phone one day, and tell myself to shut up. Miles Davis to Nat Hentoff, *The Jazz Life* (New York: The Dial Press, 1971).

The elephant . . . He is Ganesh. Charles Olson.

Subsequent wanderings on Long Island in fear of the Lord

Allen Ginsberg
April 1, 1949

What's become of my vision
         on the corner of Jack Dempsey?
I the martyr. I the obstacle.
I the evernarrowing path.
Shine on, you crazy diamond.
It's your project.

It's not me, it's the sun.
Hiding out behind the clouds.
The spiral or the speed.
The stone   or the seed.

My curmudgeon is in full swing and I am hoping to keep my paws out of the states for a time – tempting the family to head north. [1]

Epiphany at every step. [2] Like most artists, a prisoner of love. One's job, really, is to make the words flesh. [3] Hippies, bikers, and cowboys on acid.[4] He could be that. Language facilitator's prayer to the invisible people in the woods.[5] Dig not the distortion. [6]

Maybe it just feels faster because you're moving. [7]

---

1   Ben Scott Luna.
2   Milosz.
3   Peter O'Toole, interviewed by Charlie Rose.
4   Matt Meighan.
5   Phrases used by musician Matthew Shipp.
6   Duke Ellington.
7   Bill Sterr.

> **Inspiration is for amateurs.**
> **The rest of us just show up and do the work.**
> *Chuck Close*

Just utterance. The Plural vs. the Singular.
No, I be concubining.
This statement simply penetrates me. True, not real.

Soul is an Elastic Man
shrieking at God
behind an Outback Steakhouse.

One is invited to
remember and imagine
one's own Joanne.

Now go bang the sculptress.
Really penetrate.

What we desire.
May not be.
What we seek.

One is invited remember and imagine one's own Joanne. Daniel Kane, *All Poets Welcome: The Lower East Side Poetry Scene in the 1960s* (University of California Press, 2003).

Now go bang the sculptress. Lynn Alexander.

What we desire. May not be. What we seek. Judith Montgomery.

Never trust anybody who doesn't smoke pot or listen to Bob Dylan
For Dennis McBride

When I was a toddler I sat on Freud's lap.
My connection with him is from the bottom up.
He was always good for a story:

"I look at the flower, and I want to fuck it. This is sanctuary."

As he dissects space and time, a sound
like a thorn unfurling emanates from deep in Dennis's throat.
He suggests that it is a "sensory issue" in the automatic facet:

"Reality is a filthy tyrant in tight pants."

Never trust anybody who doesn't smoke pot or listen to Bob Dylan. Dr. Jeffrey Squires
in the film *The Wackness.*

Reality is a filthy tyrant in tight pants. Dennis McBride.

Reality is a filthy tyrant in tight pants
For my friends at Paper Tiger Coffee

Flirted with the paleontologist. He invited me to his penthouse. It's weird the sacrifices you make for beauty. Eyes see crazy fast. Nothing here occurs in a vacuum. William Berg saw eternity in an hour. Kind of a meandering thoughtful something. Kicks in all genres. I pleasured 23 vaginas. Jenney bitch slapped azure. My sister and I planted thought forms down the hall. "Oh shit," she mused. This image is hardened. A tool to possibly make changes. It's very abstract and complicated, I promise. Everything else is free and for your mouth.

Reality is a filthy tyrant in tight pants. Dennis McBride.

Flirted with the paleontologist. He invited me to his penthouse. Darlene Costello.

It's weird the sacrifices you make for beauty. Sunshine.

Eyes see crazy fast. Rhonda Grace.

Nothing here occurs in a vacuum. Dan Nelson.

William Berg saw eternity in an hour. Gordon.

Kind of a meandering thoughtful something. Rhonda Grace.

I pleasured 23 vaginas. Mike G.

"Oh shit," she mused. Herb Stokes.

This image is hardened. Julene Tripp Weaver.

It's very abstract and complicated, I promise. Alex Birkett.

Tod Marshall Distilled
at Vancouver School of Arts and Academics
April 27, 2017

polysyllabic mouthful person
"a fire was in my head" (W.B. Yeats)

longing for astonishment
a reset dynamic

that gesture
is absolutely ripped off
from a Robert Frost poem

there are often
stronger connections
than the rational

metaphor carries us
to a new place of
understanding

Never Can Say Goodbye
For Eric Ahern-Sawyer

You're pretty loose. Squid don't know the difference between Chthulu and a chupacabra. The actual sound – as nearly as human organs could imitate it or human letters record it – may be taken as something like Khlul'-hloo, with the first syllable pronounced gutturally and very thickly. Don't know the words to "We're Goin' to Jackson." She should get it by now. Coco offers to take us on a tour of the area strip clubs – knows where to find the best steak. I'm not going anywhere. Some kinda spatial anomaly. The best approximation one can make is to grunt, bark, or cough the imperfectly formed syllables Cluh-Luh with the tip of the tongue firmly affixed to the roof of the mouth. That is, if one is a human being. Directions for other entities are naturally different. That just proves that blondes don't have more fun – at least not in Oak Grove.

From H.P. Lovecraft's letters: "The actual sound - as nearly as human organs could imitate it or human letters record it - may be taken as something like Khlul'-hloo, with the first syllable pronounced gutturally and very thickly.

"The best approximation one can make is to grunt, bark, or cough the imperfectly formed syllables Cluh-Luh with the tip of the tongue firmly affixed to the roof of the mouth. That is, if one is a human being. Directions for other entities are naturally different."

There are ways people solve you
Brittany Baldwin

Finally found our Western groove:

> I will show the strength of laws. Man will only find truth
> when he searches for truth. Life has its laws. I don't
> believe in laws. I am eternal. I hate dramas. I already met
> you in the future, I don't need to meet you in the past.

The sky is like a painting.
Happy, with a hint of confusion. Always.
In every car there's a story.
Your ultimate identity is totally open space.
It's OK to take naps, as long as you wake up.

I don't wanna be a scumbag of the earth.
Intentionality is not my forte.
I never really thought too much about algae.
I knew him as a poet, an affliction we shared.

Finally found our Western groove. Tian.

The sky is like a painting. Happy, with a hint of confusion. Always. Angelo Luna.

In every car there's a story. Annette Ernst.

Your ultimate identity is totally open space. Allen Ginsberg.

It's OK to take naps, as long as you wake up. Eileen Elliott.

I don't wanna be a scumbag of the earth. Alex K.

Intentionality is not my forte. Dan Raphael.

I never really thought too much about algae. Kristi M.

I knew him as a poet, an affliction we shared. Rick Vrana.

The Gleaner and I

The soprano was a computer. Nothing but a cute little ruin. He never grew up. The world grew up around him. His old man was a Nihilist. A real perv. Tried to balance the streaks. Nurtured it like a serpent to his breast.

Didn't understand why I swallowed the transistor. I do like flowers and say odd things. I think it was everyone's opinion that this was a mistake that can be stopped and turned around. The world grew up around him, and buried him.

Tomorrow the discomfort index will be quite high. Some real Daniel Day-Lewis type of shit. Now you will be writing a poem for the first time in your life. Like flowers and say odd things. Live your life like a line of poetry written with a splash of blood. A world of pure potential.

The Gleaners and I is a 2000 documentary directed by Agnes Varda.

He never grew up. The world grew up around him, and buried him. Dialogue from *The Third Man.*

His old man was a Nihilist. Henry Miller, *Tropic of Cancer.*

Didn't understand why I swallowed the transistor. Steven Spielberg, in conversation with Andy Warhol.

Tomorrow the discomfort index will be quite high. Now you will be writing a poem for the first time in your life. A world of pure potential. I do like flowers and say odd things. Translated dialogue from the film *Poetry,* directed by Chang-dong Lee.

Some real Daniel Day-Lewis type of shit. Kanye West, *Rolling Stone* September 30, 2010.

Too cute to kill

He's a questioning motherfucker.
In the moment. Chewing on the divine.
As if the state were out
to destroy the subjective in each of us.
But there's a monster in his mind.
Lookin' for a real big woman to make love to.

The world is a very puzzling place.
The government took all his clothes—
flagrant, sneaking subterfuge—still
He beat it, beat it the hard way, man,
With the Rosicrucian Thing.

My Dad is not a villain.
He's just an asshole.
Like an East Coast backwoodsman.
Perpetuating the myth
That to look is to know.

Too cute to kill. Cathleen Luna's comment about her son Christopher.

Chewing on the divine. Livia Montana.

As if the state were out to destroy the subjective in each of us. Lawrence Ferlinghetti.

There's a monster in your mind. Dialogue from anime series *D-GrayMan.*

Lookin' for a real big woman to make love to. Jumpin Jack Benny.

The world is a very puzzling place. Noam Chomsky.

The government took all his clothes. Sly Stone.

Flagrant, sneaking subterfuge. Dialogue from the film *Anatomy of a Murder*.

He beat it, beat it the hard way, man, with the Rosicrucian Thing. Charles Mingus on Sonny Rollins in *Mingus Speaks* by Paul Goodman, page 300.

My Dad is not a villain. He's just an asshole. Person on the street interviewed for Brandon Stanton's *Humans of New York,* January 18, 2015.

Perpetuating the myth that to look is to know. J'Lyn Chapman.

An Assertion That Tolerates No Company

firebringer hold up
it's too early
for your righteous fury
too soon to unfurl
your karmic surprise

Reversals address displacement and linkage.
The contradiction and the paradox.
Entirely transcended and totally transposed.

settle into a hypnotic river of sound
haunt and be haunted

intuition is the fire
freight train your friday night nickname

Moments from a fatality,
Keeper of the Secret Heart of Rivers proclaims:
There's more good, and there's more joy,
and there's more happiness in life than
there is the opposite. And it will be back.

[A painting is] an assertion that tolerates no company. Gerhard Richter.

Reversals....highly related. Kerstin Bratsch.

Settle into a hypnotic river of sound. Jim Morrison.

Haunt and be haunted. Alec Matthews.

Moments from a fatality. Jae Luna.

Keeper of the secret heart of rivers. Lori Loranger's comment on the author.

There's more good....It will be back. Roman Catholic Bishop David O'Connell.

I will try to italicize my voice
Kathleen Flenniken

The time for subterfuge is past. I am an armature. I do like flowers and say odd things. Have quite simply forgotten the name of my universe. An invisible party hides around human beings. An alchemy in the margin. Enormous, visible or conspicuous or at any rate, underlying. Hope and doubt linked forever in dance. So I blow them up with love.

The time for subterfuge is past.... I blew them up with love. Dialogue from *Doctor Who.*

I am an armature. Donna Roberge.

I do like flowers and say odd things. Translated dialogue from the film *Poetry,* directed by Chang-dong Lee.

I had quite simply forgotten the name of my universe. Carl Solomon.

There is an alchemy in the margin. Sage Cohen.

Intend to Attend

A beautiful chaos, this life. A world of pure potential. Tomorrow the discomfort index will be quite high. The weight of too many goddamn outbursts strung around my neck like an albatross. Ghost glimpsed at the periphery. Undefined blur caught by insufficient retina. Fractals behind the eyes. The moment's gonna get you. Nurture it like a serpent to your breast. Like a neutron caterwaul. Moments away from a fatality. Skeleton falling apart. Filled with the seeds of all the troubles and blessings of existence, but also provided with the sustaining virtue, hope.

Intend to attend. Herb Stokes.

A beautiful chaos, this life. Vishal Khanna.

A world of pure potential. Translated dialogue from the film *Poetry*, directed by Chang-dong Lee.

The weight of too many goddamn outbursts strung around my neck like an albatross. Leah Noble Davidson.

Fractals behind his eyes. Doug Marx.

The moment's gonna get you. Wayne Shorter.

Like a neutron caterwaul. Katharine Salzmann.

Moments away from a fatality. Jae Luna.

His skeleton was falling apart. Daniel Skach-Mills.

Filled with the seeds of all the troubles and blessings of existence, but also provided with the sustaining virtue, hope. Joseph Campbell, *The Hero with a Thousand Faces*, p. 23.

We'll Tower While We Can
An Ode to Mike G.

Courageous. Engaged. A true friend, possessed of genuine compassion. Trying harder than most to put his shit in order. Don't fuck with the laws of nature. Got a funny soul. Blows like Charlie Parker. Loving, even when screaming righteous indignation at the gods. Too cute to kill. "Everyone's concerned with their stupid money." Mike G's heart is big enough to save the sad sad world from the class system.

Nobody really knows how to deal with the unexpected. How do you rehearse the unknown? If I feel I'm in the Tower of Terror, a little piece will just let me breathe. The sky becomes like a painting. Happy, with a hint of confusion. Vulnerable, put upon, suffering, defiantly and unapologetically optimistic, Mike G. does not stand down.

Got a funny soul. He plays like Charlie Parker. Charles Mingus.

Too cute to kill. Cathleen Luna's comment about Christopher Luna, following his apology for being a pain in her ass as a kid.

Nobody really know how to deal with the unexpected. How do you rehearse the unknown? Wayne Shorter.

If I feel I'm in the Tower of Terror, a little piece will just let me breathe. Lena Dunham.

The sky is like a painting. Happy, with a hint of confusion. Angelo Luna.

His skeleton was falling apart

Three lovely lesbians
were discussing Pompeii.
Fondling the subject.

All of a sudden it's dirty, messy,
and redolent of language power.

To haunt and be haunted.
All my success I owe to them
who cleansed me and showed me the way.

If I feel I'm in the Tower of Terror,
a little piece will just let me breathe.

Moments away from a fatality,
I stand with the grasshoppers.

I said yes, and it was lovely.
The rules don't permit it; I permit it.

His skeleton was falling apart. Daniel Skach-Mills.

Three lovely lesbians were discussing Pompeii. Kristopher Molina.

Fondling the subject. All of a sudden it's dirty, messy. Josh Ehrdal.

Redolent of language power. Dan Raphael.

To haunt and be haunted. Alec Matthews.

If I feel I'm in the Tower of Terror, a little piece will just let me breathe. Lena Dunham.

Moments away from a fatality. Jae Luna.

I stand with the grasshoppers. Jenney Pauer.

I said yes, and it was lovely. Grace Valentine.

The rules don't permit it; I permit it. Beethoven.

I burn dandelions
Aaron Pacora

Circumstance leads kid into the tall grass, from which he must extricate his bicycle, hoping no one was looking. Fate's the great arranger none are the master of. Because I am a monkey I must have bananas. Pile them high. Need a moment? Take one. The prostitution planets are aligning.

Memory slippery as God. Grass covers all. Not lotion. Lotioning. I think I've discovered innocence. It's over there. We should check it out. What did you hear? Transcendence of material fact into a realm of luminous deliverance. I'm gonna have to work on that if I'm gonna trot these pieces out. Leave a trail of bodies to lead us out of the maze and into the sunlight again.

Fate's the great arranger none are the master of. Herb Stokes.

Because I am a monkey, I must have bananas. Overheard at Vancouver School of Arts and Academics, May 12, 2014.

The prostitution planets are aligning. John Cameron Mitchell.

Grass covers all....Pile them high. Carl Sandburg.

*Not lotion. Lotioning. I'm gonna have to work on that....*Michelle Fredette.

I think I've discovered innocence. It's over there. We should check it out. Lena-Lee in the anime *D-Gray Man.*

Transcendence of material fact into a realm of luminous deliverance. R.C. Baker on Mark Rothko.

Stay outta the churches, son
William S. Burroughs

Life is a mosaic, and my [poem] is one little piece. The movie of life is a kaleidoscopic time lapse of co-creation. [Think] deeply about every word, every gesture, yet [leave] space for spontaneous combustion. [Avoid] confrontations and ego struggles. Fate's the great arranger none are the master of. Your most formidable enemy lies within yourself. The vibration of love can change your DNA, you know. It's tonality. Like, the tone changes from second to second... it's like... chaos! I'm just totally here in the moment, you know? Drawing the power of life! Did you know the power of life actually makes geometric patterns on the earth? The power actually moves... not like it does on the sun, you know... but still! It's EPIC. I see what the animals see. Fear doesn't necessarily go away, but you befriend it. There's an endless question about what everything is made of. It's all a movie, including this conversation. There's no answer to it.

Life is a mosaic, and my [poem] is one little piece. The movie of life is a kaleidoscopic time lapse of co-creation. Pharrell Williams.

He thinks deeply about every word, every gesture, yet leaves space for spontaneous combustion. He avoids confrontations and ego struggles. Director Philip Noyce on actor Jeff Bridges.

Fate's the great arranger none are the master of. Herb Stokes.

Your most formidable enemy lies within yourself. Dialogue from the film *Jet Li's Fearless.*

The vibration of love....I see what the animals see. "Super Cute Hippie Chick" interviewed by Wm. Steven Humphrey for the *Portland Mercury*, July 31, 2014.

Fear doesn't necessarily go away, but you befriend it. Jeff Bridges, interviewed by *AARP the Magazine,* August/September 2014.

There's an endless question about what everything is made of. It's all a movie, including this conversation. There's no answer to it. Harry Dean Stanton in *Partly Fiction.*

The Fragility of the Eagle

Chickens heed the split tongue of the prodigal son.
Piece of shit flying around with a halo.

Shunned crackpots. They could do whatever they wanted. Being
godlike. Sometimes the evil just come out.

Bullshit division. Holding yourself back from
understanding the universe.

Dismemberment is not cool.
What is is? Deconstruction of self.

There is an alchemy in the margin. The release of constraints.
Boil down what is left. Filter out unwanted parts.

Unconscious female. Most perfect being. Most perfect substance.
The Essence. The One. Ambrosia in the brain makes you immortal.
The third eye, you open it. Basically, you are existing on all levels
of reality.

The Fragility of the Eagle. Kevin Killian, misspeaking a line from his book, *Spread Eagle* at Embers, Portland, OR May 30.

Shunned crackpots...Being godlike....Holding yourself back. Deconstruction of the self....Basically, you are existing on all levels of reality. Nathan Gilcrease.

Dismemberment is not cool. Kelley Clifton.

What is is? Chelsea Davis.

There is an alchemy in the margin. Sage Cohen.

This is a deeply personal business, and it demands respect
Bruce Springsteen

This Professor Lorenz is a hypnotist as well as a horticulturalist. It's a geography of the spirit for him. Writing this thing on communicating with the divine spirits. A million birds came to [the] window. . . Felt he was on the same beam, man, tuned in the same. Millions of birds, man. What they really pay you for is to be as present and alive as you can be. We create the illusion of stasis. You've got to destroy that mattress. It has to be rebirth on a nightly basis.

This Professor Lorenz is a hypnotist as well as a horticulturalist. Dialogue from *The Corpse Vanishes*, 1942.

It's a geography of the spirit for him. Shelby Reece.

Writing this thing....millions of birds, man. Charles Mingus.

We create the illusion of stasis. Narration spoken by spoken Jake (David Mazouz), the brilliant troubled child in the 2012-2013 TV program *Touch*.

You've got to destroy that mattress. Dialogue spoken by Kirsty Cotton, the female protagonist played by Ashley Laurence in the 1988 horror film *Hellbound: Hellraiser II*.

secret accountability is a terrible contradiction

I have spent aeons
sitting here
right here

a black hole
a soulless, evil
piece of shit

naturally, this country can't stand truth
I knew my voice could kill people
so it was better not to speak

a spinsterish obsession
no intention of making my life a bore
with precautions of this sort

had to hold my daughter
& crush her head so
she could go up
to the sky

He's a black hole. He is a soulless, evil piece of shit. Michael Shannon on Donald Trump, November 29, 2016.

Naturally, this country can't stand truth. Louis Michaux.

I knew my voice could kill people, so it was better not to speak. Maya Angelou.

A spinsterish obsession. No intention of making my life a bore with precautions of this sort. Simone Du Beauvoir, *New York Times*, October 13, 2016.

I had to hold my daughter and crush her head so she could go up to the sky. Kyle Stephen Brian Holder, accused of beating his two-year-old daughter nearly to death in a hotel in Salmon Creek, Vancouver, WA.

You Can't Fight the Threads of Fate

I have no complaints. I've had a good life, you know. Lots of adventures. It's had some dark parts, too, but mainly I've had a pretty good run of it, and I don't want to cling too hard. Every dramatic life force in us rises to win the fullness of our life when Death itself challenges. I think I've discovered innocence. It's over there. We should check it out. There's an endless question about what everything is made of. It's all a movie, including this conversation. There's no answer to it.

You can't fight the threads of fate. Nui Harime in the anime *Kill La Kill (The Woman With the Scissor Blade).*

I have no complaints….I don't want to cling too hard. Peter Matthiessen.

Every dramatic life force in us rises to win the fullness of our life when Death itself challenges. Robert Duncan to Helen Adam, quoted in Lisa Jarnot's *Robert Duncan, The Ambassador from Venus: A Biography* (University of California Press, 2012), page 211.

I think I've discovered innocence. It's over there. We should check it out. Lena-Lee in the anime *D-Gray Man.*

There's an endless question about what everything is made of. It's all a movie….no answer to it. Harry Dean Stanton in *Partly Fiction.*

No One Wants to be Accused of Paying Attention to the Wrong Things
J'Lyn Chapman

Behold the power of my freed ego. Dropping shards of love. You can live life the way you always imagined it would play out, or you can try to make the thing you dream of making. If you choose the second, get ready for an amazing ride. That's the ride I'm on. I realize that it must seem like the greatest arrogance to think one could escape life's mundane concerns, like asking to live on a cloud, floating above the mere mortals. That sort of arrogance…is the only thing that's gotten me anywhere in life. I'm just giving you a little taste of my energy right now. I'm not even full-fledged. I've seen a lot of miracles. You can say that I'm a little bit of a holy man. I never made any vow to poetry except to cut its throat, if I could make someone laugh. A poem knows where you already are, and it nails you there.

Behold the power of my freed ego. Ira Gamagoori in the anime *Kill La Kill (The Woman with the Scissor Blade).*

Dropping shards of love. Patti Smith, "Tarkovsky."

You can live life the way you always imagined it would play out, or you can try to make the thing you dream of making. If you choose the second, get ready for an amazing ride. That's the ride I'm on. Rei Kawakubo, founder of Comme des Garcon.

I'm just giving you a little taste of my energy right now. I'm not even full fledged. You can say that I'm a little bit of a holy man. I've seen a lot of miracles. Man interviewed for Brandon Stanton's *Humans of New York.*

I realize that it must seem like the greatest arrogance to think one could escape life's mundane concerns, like asking to live on a cloud, floating above the mere mortals. That sort of arrogance…is the only thing that's gotten me anywhere in life. Hacktivist Aaron Swartz, *New York*, February 18-23, 2013.

I never made any vow to poetry except to cut its throat, if I could make someone laugh. Robert Duncan, according to George Stanley, in Lisa Jarnot's *Robert Duncan, The Ambassador from Venus: A Biography* (University of California Press, 2012), page 219.

A poem knows where you already are, and it nails you there. William Stafford.

Reciprocity is in the House
An Entirely Happy Convergence

Our thoughts have forms. It's all a movie, including this conversation. There's no answer to it. Sometimes I reference people, or the stars, the sun, the moon, and universal interstellar space type shit. But then she looks at me with those eyes. She punches me in the physics and I realize that we are filled with the seeds of all the troubles and blessings of existence, but also provided with the sustaining virtue, hope.

You don't see any magic? Here on the streets is action. It is the necromantical numina of the netherworld we are courting. It's exciting. Very large. A nonhuman, abstract dance, a war of elements, torn, resoldered percussion gestures. It is the fecund labyrinth again, with so many rooms, cells, vibrations, percussions, repercussions.

I have not been as others were. I've seen a lot of miracles. I'm just giving you a little taste of my energy right now. I'm not even full-fledged. I think I've discovered innocence. Lips touch soft my rim. When you see them with space between them, they are phenomenal specks of light. Let's not become robots, and forget our fellow man. Applaud all songs. If crows were robots, I'd love them just the same. I think to love bravely is best, and accept as much as you can bear.

Reciprocity is in the house. Yugen Rashad, KBOO Radio Portland, OR.

It's entirely a happy convergence. Patti Smith.

Our thoughts have forms. Dialogue from the anime series *D-Gray Man.*

It's all a movie....no answer to it. Harry Dean Stanton in *Partly Fiction.*

Sometimes I reference people. ... But then she looks at me with those eyes. Nathaniel Russell.

She punched me in the physics. Matt Eiford-Schroeder.

Filled with the seeds of all the troubles and blessings of existence, but also provided with the sustaining virtue, hope. Joseph Campbell, *The Hero with a Thousand Faces* (Princeton University Press, 1973), p. 23.

You don't see any magic? David Choe.

Here on the streets is action. David Meltzer.

It was the necromantical numina of the netherworld we were courting. Tom Robbins, after ingesting magic mushrooms, from *Tibetan Peach Pie* (Ecco, 2014), page 58.

A nonhuman...repercussions. Anaïs Nin on Robert Duncan, from Lisa Jarnot's *Robert Duncan, The Ambassador from Venus: A Biography* (University of California Press, 2012) , page 76.

I have not been as others were. Edgar Allan Poe.

I've seen a lot of miracles. I'm just giving you a little taste of my energy right now. I'm not even full-fledged. Man interviewed for Brandon Stanton's *Humans of New York.*

I think I've discovered innocence. Lena-Lee in the anime *D-Gray Man.*

Lips touch soft my rim. Roxanne Bash.

When you see them with space between them, they are phenomenal specks of light. Space, interviewed by Brandon Stanton for *Humans of New York.*

Let's not become robots, and forget our fellow man. Yusef Lateef.

Applaud all songs. e.e. cummings.

If crows were robots, I'd love them just the same. Mike G.

I think to love bravely is best, and accept as much as you can bear. Marilyn Monroe.

You Cannot Stop the Onslaught of My Mighty Love
Lori Loranger

Messiah of evil. Mind like a labyrinth. The Leopard. The All Star. The Devotee. A horrifying perfection. Has her full attention. It's not vitamins she needs. Here's a little slide show. Balance. On the rice fields. In conversation souls merge, cross-pollinate. Third pathway observes, taking copious notes.

Jesus speaks to her through iambic pentameter. Humping plurality. Sodomizing duality. All kinds of unknown things could go wrong. And do. Poem knows where you already are, and it nails you there. Mutate time really. It's entirely a happy convergence.

Nature doesn't give a fuck, man. They got lava bitches here. It's a biohazard. It's chunky. The books can't help me to kill the devil. Sometimes she still has those tendencies.

"I don't want your judgment. I don't wanna freak out about it, but I heard it was pretty bad."

"I have no identity. Lost forever in you. Why do I do it? Why do I come here? How can my mind become peaceful?"

"You must retain the mind of kindness."

The odd bedfellows one does keep when he is dead. No one wants to be accused of paying attention to the wrong things. It is strange living in a place where people are soul sick. If you're willing to be puzzled, you can learn.

A horrifying perfection. Patti Smith.

Jesus speaks to her through iambic pentameter. Michelle Giuliano.

Humping plurality. Matt Eiford.

All kinds of unknown things could go wrong. Holly Black.

A poem knows where you already are, and it nails you there. William Stafford.

Mutate time really. Jimmy Page.

It's entirely a happy convergence. Patti Smith.

Nature doesn't give a fuck, man. Charles Bukowski.

They got lava bitches here. Old Dirty Bastard.

It's a biohazard. It's chunky. Jane Arnal.

The books can't help me to kill the devil. How can my mind become peaceful? You must retain the mind of kindness. Translated dialogue from the film *Shaolin vs. Lama*, 1983.

I have no identity. Lost forever in you. Why do I do it? Why do I come here? It's not vitamins she needs. The odd bedfellows one does keep when he is dead. Dialogue from the film *Girl on a Motorcycle*, starring Marianne Faithfull.

No one wants to be accused of paying attention to the wrong things. J'Lyn Chapman.

It is strange living in a place where people are soul sick. Benicio del Toro as James Picard in the film *Jimmy P.*

If you're willing to be puzzled, you can learn. Noam Chomsky, interviewed by Michel Gondry for the film *Is the Man Who Is Tall Happy?*

Your heart is as big as the world
Paul Yates

I am a soldier, a medic
performing an autopsy
on your broken soul.

Waist-deep in an autoclave.
All sorts of past demise.
I ejaculate red, white, and blue.
It's not sanity; even if you high,
this shit don't sound sane.

Where are the helpful hordes?
Have they got some sort of social anxiety disorder?

I remember how transforming it was to feel that I was loved.

How does one disable speech?

Jim Morrison read Rimbaud,
Nietzsche's *Birth of Tragedy*,
and Joseph's Campbell's *Hero of a Thousand Faces*.
I want to know what the fuck moved him to do those things.

I don't wanna be rich.
"Starving artist," that's legit.

And now for some real gore. Dying to oneself.
The vocabulary of the mystics. An entirely happy convergence.
A geography of the spirits for me.

The world is a very puzzling place.
If you're willing to be puzzled, you can learn.

Our sweet, blind, bottomless hope.
Took too long to get here; still glad
I made the journey.

Your heart is as big as the world. Filmmaker Paul Yates's opinion of the author.

I am a soldier, a medic performing an autopsy on your broken soul. Angelo Luna.

All sorts of past demise. Dan Luna.

I ejaculate red, white, and blue. Greg Luna, b. July 4, 1976.

It's not sanity...I want to know, etc. The RZA, on the news that Andre "Christ Bearer" Johnson of the California duo Northstar had cut off his penis and attempted suicide by jumping from his second story balcony.

Where are the helpful hordes? Musician Sari Breznau, waiting in vain for assistance moving her equipment before a house party.

I remember how transforming it was to feel that I was loved. David James Randolph.

I don't wanna be rich. "Starving artist," that's legit. Student overheard outside the Vancouver School of Arts and Academics.

Dying to oneself. The vocabulary of the mystics. Joseph Campbell, in conversation with Bill Moyers, *The Power of Myth* (Anchor, 1991), page 112.

It's entirely a happy convergence. Patti Smith.

It's a geography of the spirits. Shelby Reece.

The world is a very puzzling place. If you're willing to be puzzled, you can learn. Noam Chomsky, interviewed by Michel Gondry for the film *Is the Man Who Is Tall Happy?*

Our sweet, blind, bottomless hope. Kristin Berger.

A need that masquerades itself
Livia Montana

Seemed like everyone, even the moon, was happy and drunk. Somewhere in every intellectual is a dumb prick. I realize that it must seem like the greatest arrogance to think one could escape life's mundane concerns, like asking to live on a cloud, floating above the mere mortals. That sort of arrogance…is the only thing that's gotten me anywhere in life.

Eat this deadly technique. Sublime and beautiful. Raw and painful. So pure and unfiltered. The howling sound of sorrow. Ugly. Dangerous. Particles of chaos. Omnivorous mind devours everything.

Every once in a while, my own genius overwhelms me. Like a Greek moving van, memorable speech [goes] past the anecdote. A poem knows where you already are, and it nails you there. Jars you into empathy. A lifetime of mediated experience. Finite number of words. Infinite number of possibilities.

I'll do Truth and Beauty. To incorporate the two is the work of a cosmic wisdom. This heinous implement. Wholesome and delightful. An unfolding permission to stroll freely. To become a nonentity. When you disappear, fear disappears with you. The storehouse of optimism is replenished. The universe is a wondrous thing. I shall cogitate upon it.

Seemed like everyone, even the moon, was happy and drunk. Lidia Yuknavitch.

Somewhere in every intellectual is a dumb prick. Sandor Himmelstein.

I realize that it must seem like the greatest arrogance to think one could escape life's mundane concerns, like asking to live on a cloud, floating above the mere mortals. That sort of arrogance...is the only thing that's gotten me anywhere in life. Aaron Swartz, *New York*, February 18-23, 2013.

Eat this deadly technique. Translated dialogue from the anime *Kaze No Stigma.*

Sublime and beautiful. Raw and painful. Ugly. Dangerous....A finite number of words. An infinite number of possibilities. Wendell Pierce.

So pure and unfiltered. Laura Sciortino.

The howling sound of sorrow.... Particles of chaos.... This heinous implement.... To become a nonentity.... The universe is a wondrous thing. I shall cogitate upon it. Dialogue from Mike Leigh's film *Mr. Turner.*

Omnivorous mind devours everything. Lawrence Ferlinghetti.

Every once in a while, my own genius overwhelms me. Patti Smith.

Memorable speech [goes] past the anecdote. Jars you into empathy. Elizabeth Austen.

A poem knows where you already are, and it nails you there. William Stafford.

Launched into a lifetime of mediated experience. Rebecca Wolff.

I'll do Truth and Beauty. Karen Read.

To incorporate the two is the work of a cosmic wisdom. Eliot Weinberger.

Wholesome and delightful. Matt Eiford-Schroeder.

An unfolding permission to stroll freely. Morgan Hutchinson.

When you disappear, fear disappears with you. David Meltzer.

The storehouse of optimism is being replenished. Sabra Larsen.

Even More Words of Advice for Young People

You shouldn't get old.
You shouldn't drink too much.
So stay young. Don't drink too much.

Retrace your own pain
with a lot of liberty and recklessness.

You're fine.
It's the rest of the world
That's delusional.

Never walk over a writer . . .
unless you're positive he can't rise up behind you.
If you're going to burn him, make sure he's dead.
Because if he's alive, he will talk:
talk in written form, on the printed, permanent page.

You shouldn't get old....Don't drink too much. Walt Curtis, at Three Friends Coffee House, Portland, OR February 23, 2009.

You're fine. It's the rest of the world that's delusional. Captain Jack Harkness, in *Torchwood.*

Retrace your own pain.... liberty and recklessness. Shawn Sorensen.

Never walk over a writer . . . . on the printed, permanent page. Philip K. Dick, *Radio Free Albemuth* (Avon Books, 1985).

We're gonna find out the fate of humanity
Liz Donley

The boy, the beast, and the butterfly
Walk across a bridge of magpies
Dropping shards of love
All so pure and unfiltered.

A whole new side to the Luna mythos:
Freedom within form.
Sublime and beautiful.
Raw and painful. And ugly.
Dangerous. Made me wish for a village.

The little me that wanted to be a painter.
Launched into a lifetime of mediated experience.

> I have to believe everything in order to make stuff up.
> A literacy of the heart. Finite number of words. Infinite
> number of possibilities. An irresistible mix of art and
> genitals. Brings that transcendence into our lives. Teaches
> us how to feel, what our parameters can be, what sensations
> can be like. Makes us more engaged with life.

I've been in a perpetual dither of late.
It's the guy I've been bangin.
See, I'm the star of a one-woman/multi-
            man variety show.
Life is crazy blurry sometimes.
A tsunami of disease-free tomorrows
come flooding my way.

There's no such thing as things as they are.
I always wanted to see more.
If one can understand love, one can be,
to a certain extent, fearless.

The boy, the beast, and the butterfly. . . . Walk across a bridge of magpies. . . . Dropping shards of love. Patti Smith, from "Tarkovsky."

All so pure and unfiltered. Laura Sciortino.

A whole new side to the Luna mythos. Miles Hewitt.

Freedom within form. Sublime and beautiful. Raw and painful. And ugly. Dangerous.... A finite number of words. An infinite number of possibilities. Wendell Pierce.

It made me wish for a village. Karen Read.

The little me that wanted to be a painter. Rowan Ricardo Phillip.

Launched into a lifetime of mediated experience. Rebecca Wolff.

I have to believe everything in order to make stuff up. Dialogue spoken by Harvey Keitel's character in the film *Youth.*

A literacy of the heart. Former Washington State Poet Laureate Samuel Green.

An irresistible mix of art and genitals. Helen Mirren on the film *Caligula.*

Brings that transcendence into our lives. Teaches us how to feel, what our parameters can be, what sensations can be like. Makes us more engaged with life. Jeff Koons, *Interview* December 12, 2012.

I've been in a perpetual dither of late. It's the guy I've been bangin. Life is crazy blurry sometimes. Barbara Lynn Cantone, gmail chat.

See, I'm the star of a one-woman/multi-man variety show. James Franco.

That a tsunami of disease-free tomorrows would come flooding her way. Dean Haspiel, from *Beef with Tomato.*

There's no such thing as things as they are. I always wanted to see more. If one can understand love, one can be, to a certain extent, fearless. David Hockney, as interviewed in the documentary *Hockney.*

Discipline was not his bag

I've been in a perpetual dither of late. It's the guy I've been
bangin. See, I'm the star of a one-woman/multi-man variety show.
A liminal figure who can pass between worlds.

Abide by your grind.
Dust his little heart.
Offer turquoise.

Life is crazy blurry sometimes. A vortex of possibilities.
Ambient photons bouncing around the room.
A mathematical transformation of each face,
encoding it in "face space." That's what you get
for making out with horrible people.

I like to be the bitch in the back. Not just an arbitrary snail.
A polysyllabic tendency. Telling the truth in a way
that makes people laugh, live, and love.

The bronze lady and the stone man
Seldom seen as anything other than sentient sledge-hammers.
Tools to crush proles into fine defeated powder.
Particles of chaos. Post-crematorium has beens or never was.
Ask many questions and get many answers.

There's a mythological aspect
            to rampant seriality.
There's a lot of
            scatological and puerile language.
An expansion of happiness
            only the valiant can create.

                    People get what they need.
                    Enough to get them through.

Discipline was not his bag. Jimmy Stewart.

I've been in a perpetual dither of late. It's the guy I've been bangin. Life is crazy blurry sometimes. Barbara Lynn Cantone, gmail chat.

See, I'm the star of a one-woman/multi-man variety show. James Franco.

A liminal figure who can pass between worlds. Molly Haskell on Sidney Poitier.

Abide by your grind. Barista Dane.

Dust his little heart. Terri Eliof.

I'll offer turquoise. Gwendolyn Morgan, at Tod Marshall's workshop at Vancouver Community Library, April 27, 2017.

A vortex of possibilities. Carlos Santana on John Coltrane, interviewed for the documentary *Chasing Trane.*

Ambient photons bouncing around the room. J. R. Burkett.

I like to be the bitch in the back. Tiffany Burba-Schramm.

Not just an arbitrary snail. Sara Pegarella.

Particles of chaos. Dialogue from Mike Leigh's film *Mr. Turner.*

Only the valiant can create. Frank Capra.

The quantity of his words increased as daylight decreased
David Meltzer (No Eyes: For Lester Young)

I hate it when unforeseen shit happens, except when I don't. That's just the Earth on fire. Nature doesn't give a fuck, man. One day it will completely collapse. I'm trying to figure out which day. It's very hard to figure out. The world is a very puzzling place. If you're willing to be puzzled, you can learn.

There are those who don't have your best interests at heart.
It's too bad we can't all be just 'predators of sweetness and light.'

Don't bleed in front of the bear. You are a future changer. A really accommodating religion. I think I'll be the Buddha of this place. We all have this channeling, this shamanistic ability. Some make more use of it than others. You have to have hubris in this world. We don't have any answers to these questions, and we don't want them. We don't need them, we just need to do the work.

That's just the Earth on fire. Devon Panosh.

Nature doesn't give a fuck, man. Charles Bukowski.

One day it will completely collapse. I'm trying to figure out which day. It's very hard to figure out. Artist Ai Wei Wei, in the documentary *The Fake Case.*

The world is a very puzzling place. If you're willing to be puzzled, you can learn. Noam Chomsky.

There are those who don't have your best interests at heart. Wendell Pierce.

It's too bad we can't all be just 'predators of sweetness and light.' Lawrence Ferlinghetti, interviewed by David Meltzer in *San Francisco Beat: Talking with the Poets.*

Don't bleed in front of the bear. John Irving.

A really accommodating religion. Selina Suit

I think I'll be the Buddha of this place. Gary Snyder.

We all have this channeling, this shamanistic ability. Some make more use of it than others. You have to have hubris in this world. We don't have any answers to these questions, and we don't want them. We don't need them, we just need to do the work. Patti Smith.

Always Naked: A Constellation Prize

We all have this channeling, this shamanistic ability. Some make more use of it than others. Every once in a while, my own genius overwhelms me. I got secrets, cousin. Constellations being lit by the subject matter. When you see them with space between them, they are phenomenal specks of light. But so many things become less certain. Somewhat conundrous. We don't have any answers to these questions, and we don't want them. We don't need them, we just need to do the work. You've got to understand your limitations. It's your limitations that make you the wonderful disaster you most probably are. You don't choose what you fear. It chooses you. You have to have hubris in this world. There are people who will try to strip you of your humanity. There are those who don't have your best interests at heart. Be fine I know you will.

I am always naked. Tiffany Burba.

A constellation prize. We all have this channeling, this shamanistic ability. Some make more use of it than others. Every once in a while, my own genius overwhelms me. We don't have any answers to these questions, and we don't want them. We don't need them, we just need to do the work....You have to have hubris in this world. Patti Smith.

I got secrets, cousin. Benicio del Toro as James Picard in the film *Jimmy P.*

Constellations being lit by the subject matter.... But so many things become less certain. Robert Downey Jr.

When you see them with space between them, they are phenomenal specks of light. Space, interviewed by Brandon Stanton for *Humans Of New York.*

Somewhat conundrous question. Dialogue from Mike Leigh's film *Mr. Turner.*

You've got to understand your limitations, etc.....You most probably are. Nick Cave, in the film *20,000 Days on Earth.*

You don't choose what you fear. It chooses you. John Irving.

There are people who will try to strip you of your humanity. There are those who don't have your best interests at heart. Wendell Pierce.

I love every movement

there's got to be more to this
tradition of transmission
than elitism and intellectual circle jerk

the tyranny of intentionality
visions of a glamorous hell
with his bags full of havoc

like Bobby and Joanie
walkin' the festival grounds
cracking a bullwhip: superstars in our thinking

there's so much to cut through
it's a very complicated terrain
where you swim, she drowns

Williams modeled brevity and precision
Duncan invited us to return to the field
Ginsberg recommended candor
Nikki reminded us to stand up

The whole impossibility of actually seeing something.
the solid marrying the liquid
that curious, lurking something

It's up to us to find
their breath in the fog
to quietly float is a huge challenge

To get people to use their eyes
and to get them to notice the things
they don't pay attention to

Everybody does look,
it's just a question of
how hard.

I love every movement. Everybody does look, it's just a question of how hard. David
Hockney, as interviewed in the documentary *Hockney*.

Tyranny of intentionality. Christopher Howell.

Visions of a glamorous hell. George Kuchar on the films of Jack Smith.

*There's so much to cut through....It's a very complicated terrain....The whole
impossibility of actually seeing something.* Gillian Conoley, interviewed by Tod
Marshall for *Range of the Possible* (Eastern Washington University, 2002), page 37.

Where you swim, she drowns. Carl Jung to James Joyce, about his schizophrenic
daughter.

The solid marrying the liquid, that curious, lurking something. Walt Whitman,
"Specimen Days."

It's up to us to find their breath in the fog. Edee Lemonier.

To quietly float is a huge challenge Toni Lumbrazo Luna.

*It's the job of the artist to get people to use their eyes and to get them to notice the
things they don't pay attention to.* John Baldessari.

How to shape the poetry juice that's all around you

beauty and pretty are never in the same room
one man's wail is another's lullaby
free from the curse of language, finally happy
pleasure and joy can be a weapon
like broccoli, it will do you no harm
like violence, is what we do

it's all good, knowwhatImean?
put the pieces where you may
let the mask fall, or put it on
the page will hold you

howl
(but)
don't get cocky
and you will shine
like the
brightest
bling

Contemplation of all that must be left behind. The advantage of
asceticism. Desire to shrink and expand simultaneously, to stave off
this need to lick everything. Nothing noble about being a consumer
of souls. Loudness. Come to rock and shock you. To be large, Big
in Japan without Totally Destroying Osaka. Learn to take nothing
personally, while personalizing everything. Always a third way, at
least. Return to the well, throw yourself in. Swim in the eddy of
words rather than the landfill of perpetual baked goods. Only you
can set yourself free. Take a leap into the void, into a river of

re   vision

delicious

a very beautiful place to live

The poetry juice that's all around you. Toni Lumbrazo Luna.

Beauty and pretty are never in the same room....pleasure and joy can be a weapon...like violence, is what we do. Robin Coste Lewis.

Free from the curse of language, finally happy Mike G.

Put the pieces where you may. Virginia Woolf.

The page will hold you. Lidia Yuknavitch.

revision is delicious Toni Morrison.

revision is a beautiful place to live Robin Coste Lewis.

The This Is Extra
Peter Matthiessen

We were turning in a dangerous rootless limitless space. In search of real breakfast, I plunged my turbulent and tender hand into the most genital of earthly places. Found nothing in the wound but a cold gust of wind that has slipped through the slack gaps in my soul. At times, in deep space, tensions develop giving rise to bizarre emotions.

The true villain of the misdeed, who is the priest and the INITIATE. With his bags full of havoc. Human wreckage becomes an aesthetic. An aesthetic of collapse, of things not coming together.

If you're open to infinity you have a chance to regenerate yourself, and once all these circles, these circular temples regenerate themselves, they're the same old world but with a fresh new morning exhalation. The impermeable becomes permeable. Molecules obey your thoughts. You become the weather.

If you're still intact, if you're still viable, it means you've been growing somehow. That all of the impressions of life have landed and stuck somewhere. You've been able to digest them and transform them into something that you can work with and live with and carry with you. It can't be diminished, because it's supreme. The only thing is, if you don't listen to it enough, you don't hear it enough. It's when you kind of quiet down, slow things down—everything sort of settles back inside and sort of re-settles. Then, maybe you can hear something.

Let's make a poem, with blood.
And I think that soon I will know all this
very precisely, yes very precisely.

We were turning in a dangerous rootless limitless space. Patti Smith.

In search of real breakfast. Gwen Osborne.

I plunged my turbulent and tender hand into the most genital of earthly places. Found nothing in the wound but a cold gust of wind that has slipped through the slack gaps in my soul. Pablo Neruda, translated by Stephen Kessler for Barry Brukoff's *Macchu Picchu.*

At times, in deep space, tensions develop giving rise to bizarre emotions. Rosemary Leary.

The true villain of the misdeed, who is the priest and the INITIATE. First, let's make a poem, with blood. And I think that soon I will know all this very precisely, yes very precisely. Antonin Artaud, translated by Jack Hirschman.

With his bags full of havoc. Stanley Kunitz on Theodore Roethke.

Human wreckage became an aesthetic. An aesthetic of collapse, of things not coming together. Ken Jacobs on Jack Smith.

If you're open to infinity you have a chance to regenerate yourself, and once all these circles, these circular temples regenerate themselves, they're the same old world but with a fresh new morning exhalation. Matthew Shipp.

The impermeable becomes permeable. Darcy Scholts.

Molecules obey your thoughts, you know. Carlos Santana.

We became the weather. Natalie Diaz.

If you're still intact....Then, maybe, you can hear something. Bill Murray.

106

I blow you into the dazzling void
Allen Ginsberg

I speak with the authority of failure. Greed, anger, and folly have been the earmarks of my life. You start with a lot of wrong ideas about everything. I had violent passions for various pursuits usually taking the form of collecting.

Art in the beginning for me was never an avenue for self expression, it was a way for me to ally myself with heroes 'cause I couldn't make contact with God. What's your phenomenology? I think I wanna be concerned with things that are weird. Physical and metaphysical. That sounds fun. Caught between jelly beans and harbor dreams. Comparing the forces they embodied. Snatched me out of chaos. That's what this thing does. It's a time and space machine. A very nice blend of particulars. Words accumulate around the rhythm.

There are only a handful of poets who truly know *how* to read their work, who can take the audience *out there*. It's a question of looking out of yourself. Deep stenography. Seeing the particular as universal. Instants in time actually observed. Transcribing your consciousness. Crazy jagged impressions of the reporter. Pained audits of the damage… incurred as a result of … treating flesh-and-blood conflicts as clashes between allegorical opposites. All of the mystery arises out of paying attention to this moment.

That's the only way it can happen. You have to listen. You have to listen. When we're really on it, we can open the valve. Can you be a good secretary of yourself? To me it has a lot to do with getting out of the way.

There was a conscious decision in my life to be part of something dynamic and flowing, something that had a life of its own, I was just a part of it. At some point I decided not to be me but they. To do something in real time and to touch people's hearts. In eternity nothing of you will remain, so why not have fun?

This idea can continue without us. When it's working, it's a living breathing thing. Immersive. You zoom into this tiny world & it becomes galactic or immense. It's not for us to define, or enclose. Not defining it, it becomes everything. This life is extraordinary. Very mysterious business.

I blow you into the dazzling void. What's your phenomenology? Physical and metaphysical. The words accumulate around the rhythm. It's a question of looking out of yourself. Allen Ginsberg.

I speak with the authority of failure. Greed, anger, and folly have been the earmarks of my life. You start with a lot of wrong ideas about everything. All of the mystery arises out of paying attention to this moment. This life is extraordinary. Very mysterious business. Peter Mathiessen.

There are only a handful of poets who truly know how to read their work, who can take the audience out there. Jim Carroll, *Forced Entries: The Downtown Diaries 1971-1973* (Penguin Books, 1987).

Art in the beginning for me was never an avenue for self expression, it was a way for me to ally myself with heroes 'cause I couldn't make contact with God. Patti Smith, interviewed by Penny Green for *Interview*, October 1973.

I think I wanna be concerned with things that are weird. That sounds fun. There was a conscious decision in my life to be part of something dynamic and flowing, something that had a life of its own, I was just a part of it. Jerry Garcia, in the film *Long Strange Trip.*

Caught between jelly beans and harbor dreams. Gary F. Suda.

Comparing the forces they embodied…. Pained audits of the damage he and those around him incurred as a result of his treating flesh-and-blood conflicts as clashes between allegorical opposites. "The Illness and Insight of Robert Lowell" by Dan Chiasson, *The New Yorker* March 20, 2017.

I had violent passions for various pursuits usually taking the form of collecting. Snatched me out of chaos. Robert Lowell, from "The Illness and Insight of Robert Lowell" by Dan Chiasson, *The New Yorker* March 20, 2017.

That's what this thing does. It's a time and space machine…. When we're really on it, we can open the valve. Mickey Hart in the film *Long Strange Trip*.

A very nice blend of particulars. John Stevens.

That's the only way it can happen. You have to listen. You have to listen. Phil Lesh in the film *Long Strange Trip*

To do something in real time and to touch people's hearts. Dennis McNally, speaking of Jerry Garcia in the film *Long Strange Trip*.

In eternity nothing of you will remain, so why not have fun. Bob Weir, in the film *Long Strange Trip*.

Immersive. You zoom into this tiny world & it becomes galactic or immense. Ellen Grossman.

I'm convinced of the vitality of the seed
David Randolph

My home and life's work were taken away. I escaped into the sanctuary of story. Pained audits of the damage incurred as a result of treating flesh-and-blood conflicts as clashes between allegorical opposites. It's a tether. A kind of malady. A very mysterious business. Artists don't make art. The art makes itself through us. I'm not the doer, you know. I'm just along for the ride.

Poetry is the conduit that makes things happen. It's the thing that feeds you and eats away at you; gives you life and is killing you at the same time. The energy is not to take. It's to dance with. It's about a process of becoming a container of different archetypes. It is immersive. You zoom into this tiny world and it becomes galactic or immense.

This is how I'm going to die one day, crushed under a pile of paper. Explosions notwithstanding, the soul is an illusion. It gets tiresome after a while. This predicament is a gift from God. If you get rid of the demons and the disturbing things, then the angels fly off, too. There is the possibility, in that mire, of an epiphany. The purpose of life is an expansion of happiness only the valiant can create. Telling about ourselves in the hope of being recognized as we'd like to be.

My home and life's work were taken away. Felix Rafael Cordero, a painter and photographer whose home in Puerto Rico was obliterated by Hurricane Maria.

I escaped into the sanctuary of story. Rene Denfeld.

Pained audits of the damage…incurred as a result of…treating flesh-and-blood conflicts as clashes between allegorical opposites. From "The Illness and Insight of Robert Lowell" by Dan Chiasson, *The New Yorker* March 20, 2017.

It's a tether. Barbara Engel.

A kind of malady. It's the thing that feeds you and eats away at you; gives you life and is killing you at the same time. Daniel Day-Lewis.

A very mysterious business. Peter Matthiessen.

Poetry is the conduit that makes things happen. Marianela Medrano.

Artists don't make art. The art makes itself through us. I'm not the doer, you know. I'm just along for the ride. Ezra Miller, interviewed by Erykah Badu, *Interview* November 2017.

The energy is not to take. It's to dance with. It's about a process of becoming a container of different archetypes. Tori Amos, interviewed by David Marchese for Vulture.com on November 13, 2017.

It was immersive. You zoom into this tiny world and it becomes galactic or immense. Ellen Grossman.

This is how I'm going to die one day, crushed under a mountain of paper. Rachel Maddow, interviewed by Janet Reitman, *Rolling Stone* June 29, 2017.

Explosions notwithstanding. Cynthia Nixon as Emily Dickinson in the film *A Quiet Passion.*

The soul is an illusion. It gets tiresome after a while. Harry Dean Stanton.

This predicament is a gift from God. Statement attributed to Abu Bakr al-Bagdadhi, purported leader of the Islamic State, by *Washington Post* reporter Louisa Loveluck, September 2017.

If you get rid of the demons and the disturbing things, then the angels fly off, too. There is the possibility, in that mire, of an epiphany. Joni Mitchell.

The purpose of life is an expansion of happiness. David Lynch.

Only the valiant can create. Frank Capra.

Telling about ourselves in the hope of being recognized as we'd like to be. Richard Avedon.

Welcome to Life, Motherfucker
with love for my fellow poets

appalled by the enormity
        of my self regard
there's got to be more to this
tradition of transmission
than elitism and intellectual circle jerk

the tyranny of intentionality
visions of a glamorous hell
with bags full of havoc

like Bobby and Joanie
walkin' the festival grounds
cracking a bullwhip: superstars in our thinking
where you swim, she drowns

The whole impossibility of actually seeing something.
I think that now that's a very difficult process to navigate.
There's so much to cut through. It's a very complicated terrain.

the solid marrying the liquid
that curious, lurking something

It's up to us to find
their breath in the fog

to quietly float
is a huge challenge

To get people to use their eyes
and to get them to notice the things
they don't pay attention to

Everybody does look,
it's just a question of
how hard.

Williams modeled brevity and precision
Duncan invited us to return to the field
Ginsberg recommended candor
Nikki reminded us to stand up

I am constantly voraciously reading medical texts until four or five
in the morning. I want more energy, I want more vitality, I want
more hair. I wanna snuff around and eavesdrop on people. I want
to go further, transcending time.

Life breaks all of us. Capitalism enters our central nervous systems
and gives us many levels of sickness. The antidote: Spermy poetic
language. Explosive and ejaculatory. A new way to communicate,
to participate, a new spiritual condition. If you're open to infinity,
you have a chance to regenerate yourself, and once all these
circles, these circular temples, regenerate themselves, they're the
same old world but with a fresh new morning exhalation.

I'll always be your friend, and even your poet laureate. I am not
a revolutionary, yet I feel I have something of value to say. I do
overshare. It's my way of trying to understand myself.... It creates
community when you talk about private things. It's sort of a hobby
of mine, the truth. The truth is not needed, but something is. I have
spent aeons sitting here. Right here. I have been to hell and back.
And let me tell you it was wonderful. One moment equals eternity.
That tranquility is right at the edge of the chaos.

words are sigils for the
           unutterable incomprehensible
ineffable energy coursing
through all life forms
poetic pictograms
guttural grunts toward meaning
phenomenological symbology
grand and finally, inadequate

Welcome to life, motherfucker. Cola Rum.

Tyranny of intentionality. Christopher Howell.

Visions of a glamorous hell. George Kuchar on the films of Jack Smith

Where you swim, she drowns. Carl Jung to James Joyce, about his schizophrenic daughter.

The whole impossibility of actually seeing something. I think that now that's a very difficult process to navigate. There's so much to cut through. It's a very complicated terrain. Gillian Conoley, interviewed by Tod Marshall for *Range of the Possible*, page 37.

The solid marrying the liquid, that curious, lurking something. Walt Whitman, "Specimen Days."

It's up to us to find their breath in the fog. Edee Lemonier.

To quietly float is a huge challenge Toni Lumbrazo Luna

It's the job of the artist to get people to use their eyes and to get them to notice the things they don't pay attention to. John Baldessari, in *Interview*.

Everybody does look, it's just a question of how hard. David Hockney, as interviewed in the documentary *Hockney*.

That's what I wanna do. I wanna snuff around and eavesdrop on people. Albert King, in conversation with Stevie Ray Vaughan.

Life breaks all of us. Lily Yeh.

A new way to communicate, to participate, a new spiritual condition. Ai Wei Wei.

If you're open to infinity.... a fresh new morning exhalation. I am not a revolutionary, yet I feel I have something of value to say. Capitalism enters our central nervous systems and gives us many levels of sickness. Spermy poetic language. Explosive and ejaculatory. Matthew Shipp.

I'll always be your friend, and even your poet laureate. Abel Lucas (Joaquin Phoenix) in Woody Allen's film *Irrational Man.*

I do overshare. It's my way of trying to understand myself. ... It creates community when you talk about private things. Carrie Fisher, interviewed by NPR not long before her death. www.npr.org/2016/11/28/503580112/carrie-fisher-opens-up-about-star-wars-the-gold-bikini-and-her-on-set-affair.

It's sort of a hobby of mine, the truth. Dialogue spoken by John Robie (Cary Grant) in Alfred Hitchcock's *To Catch A Thief.*

The truth is not needed, but something is. Dennis McBride.

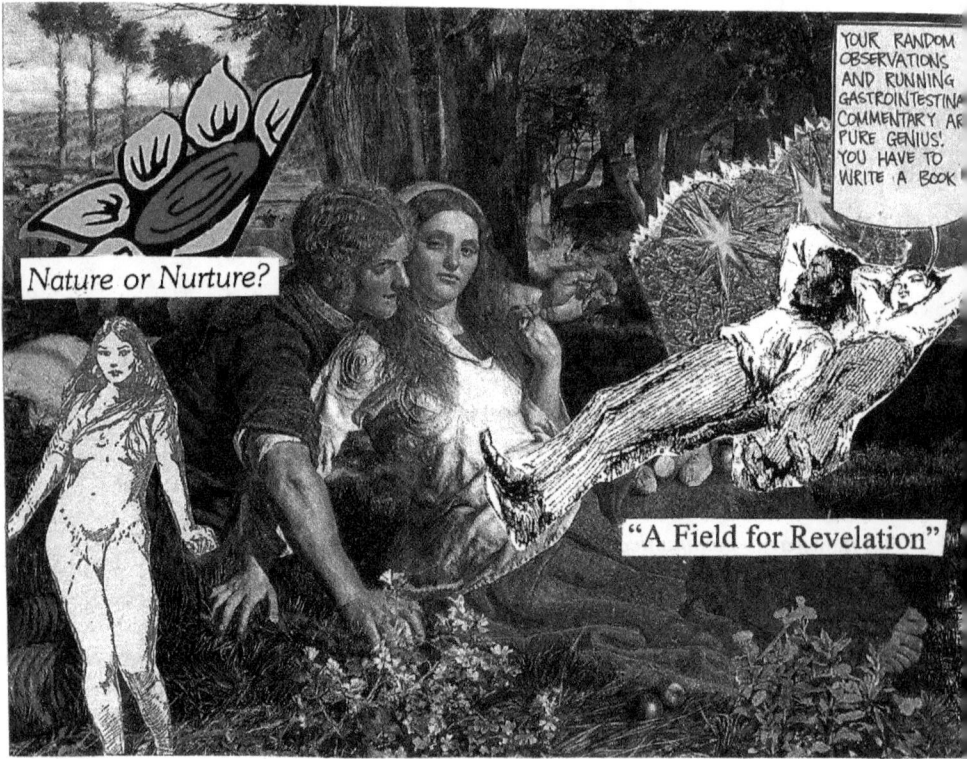

Collage Poetry: An Afterword

Provoking Vision:
Recontextualization as a Path to Self-Realization

by Christopher Luna

"The collage technique is the systematic exploitation of the accidentally or artificially provoked encounter of two or more foreign realities on a seemingly incongruous level – and the spark of poetry that leaps across the gap as these two realities are brought together." Max Ernst, 1962 https://www.modernamuseet.se/stockholm/en/exhibitions/max-ernst/ collage-frottage-grattage/

I collaged images on the outside of the black-and-white composition notebooks I used as journals for many years before I began to consider that this might be a way of making art. When I founded the Ghost Town Poetry Open Mic in 2004, I used collage on the flyers announcing the event in order to get people's attention. Later, as I became a member of the burgeoning arts community in Vancouver, WA, I created collages for local art exhibits. I also made artist trading cards, postcards, and book covers featuring my collage art for myself and others.

I had begun writing prose poetry after being introduced to the form at the Jack Kerouac School of Disembodied Poetics at Naropa University in Boulder, CO, where I earned my MFA from 1997-1999. The Kerouac School encourages what co-founder Anne Waldman has called the Outrider tradition, an umbrella term for work that does not fit easily into mainstream literature, or is created by oppressed and marginalized people. I learned rather quickly that poetry is as varied as the universe, and that the methods for creating it are limitless. It was not long before I began using found material to create prose blocks that I would come to call "collage poems."

Collage forces us out of complacency and into the liminal space where possibility resides. Here one can use allusion, dream imagery, and imaginative openness denied to some of us since childhood. Collaging can put one in a kind of trance state; furthermore, the experience of gathering, arranging, and rearranging can be a calming and even healing experience. Working with found material can help us to discard the cloak of fear and habit and break through into new discoveries. If you believe that images and words have power, then collage can be a way to practice magic and provoke the visionary.

The method is essentially recontextualization, or fracturing a text (or image) by removing one or more of its elements, then restoring order by bringing disparate linguistic (or pictorial) elements together as you assemble them in a completely new context. This act creates a spark that ignites one's consciousness. Order is forged out of chaos. New possibilities are revealed. A kind of text magic occurs in which the found material resembles the arranger, as in the poetry of the Dadaists. In fact, the new work will reflect the mind and personality of the author whether or not she intends it.

I consider a collage poem finished when it reflects my thought process, my heart, my philosophy. It can sometimes take 10-20 versions to find the correct combination of lines to accomplish this. When I find a new quotation that I love, I insert it into multiple poems-in-progress. Of course, the phrase cannot stay in all of them. It is easy to become so enamored with a line that you cannot see clearly enough to realize that it is gumming up the works. The difference between a successful and unsuccessful collage poem can be extremely subtle. Sometimes this method allows me to create surreal poetry with the dream logic associated with stream-of-consciousness writing. Recently, the poems have taken the form of collections of encouraging aphorisms aimed at inspiring poets to continue their exploration of our confounding universe.

One of the poets I met at the Kerouac School whose work had a profound impact on me was Ed Sanders. Reading his manifesto, *Investigative Poetry,* changed my life. Ed's ideas regarding opening case files on one's friends, data strips, research, and including oneself as a character in narrative poems, blew my mind. Investigative poetry seemed to integrate many of my interests—documentary film, journalism, observational narrative, collage, and cultural history—into a method for becoming a bardic scribe reporting on our endangered freedoms. Investigative poetry also lent itself nicely to my lifelong project of documenting my time on this planet. I went on to write two book-length investigative poems: *more than we can bear,* about the terrorist attacks of September 11, 2001 and their aftermath, and *Ghost Town, USA,* a decade-long chronicle of my new life in Vancouver, WA.

Anne Waldman introduced me and her other Kerouac School students to the concept of poetic lineage. Once you discover the poets who shared your approach to writing and your aesthetic concerns, you have a homework assignment for life. You are forever plugged in to a tradition as powerful as one's blood ancestry. My work finds inspiration in poet activists who believe that poetry has the power to effect social and political change: Allen Ginsberg, Nikki Giovanni, Amiri Baraka, Anne Waldman, Ed Sanders, and Diane di Prima, among others.

The poets we love give us permission to try things that we may not have been brave enough to attempt on our own. We each carry around a set of internal "rules" that were imposed upon us quite mysteriously. We learn what is possible, and are reminded of poetry's vastness, by reading the work of those who have trod this path before us.

I have been creating poems from found material since at least 1999. I first gained permission to do this without guilt from Ted Berrigan, who borrowed liberally from his friends' poems. However, I don't limit myself to lines of poetry. One of the most fruitful sources of my found poems has been the nervous chatter that poets engage in before and after they read their work to an audience. I find the comments that they make while wasting time at the mic quite fascinating and often poetic. To create the collage poems found in this book I arranged lines, recontextualizing fragments of overheard conversation, dialogue from movies, material from newspapers and magazines (especially interviews with artists and writers), and also lines from other poems.

I have received some interesting feedback on these poems from my fellow writers. Some do not believe that it is OK to borrow so freely from others. I contend that artists do this all the time, even when we are not conscious of doing so. Were one to remove allusion and homage from our great art, music, and poetry in the interest of limiting it to only that which is strictly original, we would be forced to discard most of the work that we all hold dear.

I hope that this book will provoke thought, encourage debate, and perhaps inspire a few people to relax as they continue to build on the work of their literary ancestors. Most importantly, I hope that you will experience the poems with the same sense of joy and freedom that I felt as I created them.

My deepest gratitude to the following publications for providing a home for some of the poems in this volume:

"LOVING POETRY IS LIKE BEING A FAN OF HORROR MOVIES" *Ghost Town Poetry Volume Two: 2004-2014* (Printed Matter Vancouver, 2014).

"Your Lord is a Traffic Cop" *the@tached document* #2 (Bootstrap Press, 2002).

"CATATONIC EXPRESSIONISM" *Night Bomb Review* # 2 (Fall 2010).

"The Continuing Adventures of Ecclesiastes Robinson" *Exquisite Corpse*, Issue 7. http://www.corpse.org/archives/issue_7/burning_bush/luna.htm

"magic taken seriously" *Ghost Town Poetry: Cover To Cover Books 2004-2010* (Printed Matter Vancouver, 2011).

"If any form of pleasure is exhibited, report it to me and it will be prohibited" *The Understanding Between Foxes and Light* (Great Weather for Media, 2013).

"The Mystery of Mortal Trinities: Closing Time" *On the Beam* with David Madgalene (New Way Media, 2005).

"Right Off (After Miles)" *Unshod Quills* No. 7 (March 23, 2013). https://unshodquills.wordpress.com/2013/03/23/christopher-luna/

"Message from the vessel in a dream" illustrated and printed by Subtexture (Chris Smith) for the Center for the Book Arts 2001 Broadside Series (May 2001).

"Subsequent wanderings on Long Island in fear of the Lord" Made Up Movement (2007).

"The Gleaner and I" *It's Animal But Merciful* (Great Weather for Media, 2012).

I would like to take a moment to thank some of the people who have supported and encouraged me as I worked on the poems found in this book.

First of all, I am indebted to my wife, Toni Lumbrazo Luna, a true Partner in Truth and Beauty. Toni has made our home into a sanctuary, and provides me with good advice, a sounding board, and behind-the-scenes assistance beyond measure. Before we met, I learned how miserable it is to live with someone who does not value who I am, which is equivalent to what I do. Toni has proven what is possible when two people support each other completely. She is the love of my life and the partner I was not smart enough to wish for. I am truly fortunate to have her in my corner.

I am very grateful to Michael Spring of Flowstone Press for accepting my manuscript, and for his leadership in bringing it into print. Ryan Forsythe's vision for the design of the book and its cover is greatly appreciated.

To Judith Arcana, whose mixtape poems in her Flowstone book *Announcements from the Planetarium* gave me the courage to believe that someone might someday wish to publish this manuscript containing so many poems based on found materials. Judith's poetry, activism, and spirit are a model for conscious poets to follow.

To my poetry community in Vancouver, WA and beyond for their words and their many acts of kindness. Thank you to all those who have made the Ghost Town Poetry Open Mic home since I founded it in 2004.

I am especially thankful to those who supported me before I was known for having built community through Ghost Town Poetry Open Mic, and before I was named the first Poet Laureate of Clark County, Washington. When I first arrived in the Pacific Northwest, with no contacts to speak of, I found companionship, mentoring, and venues for my work from Portland writers including David Abel, Chris Cottrell, Walt Curtis, Doug Marx, Paulann Petersen, Dan Raphael, Doug Spangle, and Joe Wheeler. I benefited from the friendship of fellow writers such as Brittany Baldwin, Sage Cohen, Amy Temple Harper, Sean Patrick Hill, and Jason Mashak.

More recently, I have received encouragement and support from Portland writers including M, Willa Schneberg, Penelope Scambly Schott, and Steve Williams. When I was new to Vancouver, I relied upon my friends and fellow writers including Diane Cammer, Eileen Elliott, Clyde Holloway, Lori Loranger, Jim Martin, Ken Palmer (RIP) and Mel Sanders. Eric Padget played trumpet with me here and in California, and introduced me to many great people from the area.

I am grateful for my students, and for those who have given me a place to present my creative writing workshops: Tracy Reilly-Kelly at Clark College, Kandy Robertson at Washington State University's Writing Center, Judith Pulman and later Amy Jo McCarville and Michael Walsh at Multnomah Arts Center, and Leah Jackson at Angst Gallery. Leah has provided a venue for poetry events since we first met in 2005, when she was the Gallery Director at Sixth Street Gallery. She also named me the poet laureate of Angst Gallery and Niche Wine Bar, allowing me to practice serving with the title for two years before the Clark County Arts Commission honored me by naming me poet laureate for the county.

A shout out to my friends and teachers from the Kerouac School, especially Antler, Jennifer Asteris, Lisa Birman, Lee Ann Brown, Tyler Burba, Natascha Bruckner, Reed Bye, John Chinworth, Jack Collom (RIP), Josepha Conrad, David Cope, Jim Cohn, Rob Ewing, Soma Feldmar, Derek Fenner, Ryan Gallagher, Allen Ginsberg (RIP), Jack Greene, Bobbie Louise Hawkins (RIP), David Henderson, Anselm Hollo (RIP), Lisa Jarnot, Vishal Khanna, Julie Kizershot, Jason Levis, David Madgalene, Matt Meighan, Todd McCarthy, Alice Notley, Shin Yu Pai, John Patsynski, Julie Patton, Akilah Oliver (RIP), Joe Richey, Randy Roark, Ed Sanders, Bill Scheffel (RIP), Michael Smoler, Steven Taylor, Totter, Lisa Trank, Saskia Wolsak, and Anne Waldman.

Finally, I'd like to thank all the people, living or dead, whose words provided material for the poems in this book. I would especially like to thank the poets and friends whose words (before, during, and after reading their work at the mic) offered such inspiration: Lynn Alexander, Jane Arnal, Elizabeth Austen, Brittany Baldwin, Roxanne Bash, Kristin Berger, Alex Birkett, Holly Black, Sari Breznau, Tiffany Burba, Barbara Lynn Cantone, J'Lyn Chapman, Sage Cohen, Darlene Costello, Walt Curtis, Leah Noble Davidson, Rene Denfeld, Natalie Diaz, Liz Donley, Josh Ehrdal, Matt Eiford, Terri Eliof, Eileen Elliott, Barbara Engel, Annette Ernst, Kathleen Flenniken, Michelle Fredette, Mike G (Michael Guimond), Rhonda Grace, Samuel Green, Jack Greene, Michelle Giuliano, Dean Haspiel, Miles Hewitt, Morgan Hutchinson, Vishal Khanna, Kevin Killian, Sabra Patricia Larsen, Rosemary Leary, Edee Lemonier, Robin Coste Lewis, Lori Loranger, Toni Lumbrazo Luna, Angelo Luna, Ben Scott Luna, Cathleen Luna, Dan Luna, Greg Luna, Jae Luna, Tod Marshall, Doug Marx, Alec Matthews, Dennis McBride, Marianela Medrano, Matt Meighan, David Meltzer (RIP), Kristopher Molina, Livia Montana, Judith Montgomery, Gwendolyn Morgan, Dan Nelson, Gwen Osborne, Aaron Pacora, Eric

Padget, Jenney Pauer, David James Randolph, Dan Raphael, Yugen Rashad, Karen Read, Shelby Reece, Donna Roberge, Katharine Salzmann, Darcy Scholts, Laura Sciortino, Daniel Skach-Mills, Michael Smoler, Shawn Sorensen, Rob Sparks, Bill Sterr, John Stevens, Herb Stokes, Gary F. Suda, Grace Valentine, Ric Vrana (RIP), Julene Tripp Weaver, Paul Yates, and Lidia Yuknavitch.

Christopher Luna is a poet, publisher, visual artist, writing coach, teacher, and editor with an MFA from the Jack Kerouac School of Disembodied Poetics at Naropa University in Boulder, Colorado. He served as Clark County, WA's first Poet Laureate from 2013-2017. He is the co-founder, with Toni Lumbrazo Luna, of Printed Matter Vancouver, an editing service and small press for Northwest writers. He and Lumbrazo Luna co-host Ghost Town Poetry Open Mic, the popular reading series he founded in 2004. He is also the editor of "The Work," a monthly email newsletter featuring poetry events in Portland, Vancouver, and the Pacific Northwest. With Luna and Lumbrazo Luna as editors, Printed Matter Vancouver published two anthologies from the series, as well as debut volumes from Clark County poets Jenney Pauer (*Serenity in the Brutal Garden*, 2012), Tiffany Burba (*Meet Me Where I Left You*, 2016), and Matthew Eiford-Schroeder (*Consistently East*, 2018).

In 2012 Luna was the subject of *Innovators of Vancouver*, one in a series of films by Chris Martin showcasing pioneering Vancouver, WA artists, business owners, and community leaders. Ghost Town Poetry Open Mic has also been featured on OPB Radio's State of Wonder.

In 2011 Niche Wine Bar and Angst Gallery proprietor Leah Jackson named him the poet laureate of her businesses. Luna teaches a monthly poetry workshop at Niche and has organized a series of bilingual poetry readings at the bar since receiving this honor. Printed Matter Vancouver and Jackson also sponsored a poetry contest to find short pieces to be printed on Niche coasters. In 2013 the Clark County Arts Commission named Luna the first Poet Laureate of Clark County, WA. He used the position to establish a Poets in the Schools program for Clark County, and he and Lumbrazo Luna partnered with Arts of Clark County to create Poetry Moves, a program that places poems by local students and adults on buses in the C-Tran system serving the county.

Luna has been a featured reader and workshop leader at Burning Word (Whidbey Island, WA), California's New Way Media Festival, Auburn Days (Auburn, WA), the Tacoma Poetry Festival (Tacoma, WA), Poets in the Park (Redmond, WA) and the Inland Poetry Prowl (Ellensburg, WA).

For more than two decades, he has collaborated with musicians including Jason Levis (Heftpistole Chamber Ensemble, Joseph's Bones, duo B.), Rob Ewing (Disappear Incompletely), Tyler Burba, Matt Meighan, Totter, Liquid Logic, Steven Taylor (the Fugs, Allen Ginsberg), and local favorites Rich and Carson Halley, Eric Padget (Future Fridays, Sigourney Reverb, Orkestar Zirconium), River Twain, Julio Appling (Trio Flux, the Student Loan), Five Guys Playing Jazz, Beth Karp, Lincoln's Beard, headshapes, David Chaparro, Caroline Chaparro, BRIZBOMB, Jim Templeton (Cosmic Dust Fusion Band), and Aram Arslanian. He has appeared on recordings by Pimpcore and Dystopia One.

"Steve Buscemi," an ode to the actor and director that Luna recorded with Dystopia One, appeared on Dr. Demento and on Vin Scelsa's "Idiot's Delight." More recently, Luna has appeared on the air on KBOO FM's Talking Earth (hosted by Walt Curtis and Barbara LaMorticella), Radio Lost and Found (hosted by Rich Lindsay), and Poetry and Everything (hosted by Judith Arcana).

Luna's poetry has appeared in publications including *Not My President: The Anthology of Dissent*, *WA 129*, *The Poeming Pigeon*, *The Other Side of Violet*, *Gobshite Quarterly*, *Clark College Phoenix*, Sharon Wood Wortman's *Big & Awesome Bridges of Portland and Vancouver*, *Bombay Gin*, *World of Change*, *Twenty Four Hours Zine*, *The Understanding Between Foxes and Light*, *Continent of Light*, *It's Animal But Merciful*, *gape-seed*, *Unshod Quills*, *Take Out*, *Night Bomb Review*, *Soundings Review*, *Chiron Review*, *Full of Crow*, *Cadillac Cicatrix*, *The Lion Speaks: An Anthology for Hurricane Katrina*, *eye-rhyme*, *Gare du Nord*, *Exquisite Corpse*, *Many Mountains Moving*, *the @tached document*, and *Big Scream*.

Luna's articles and criticism have appeared in the e-zine *Writing the Life Poetic* as well as *Rain Taxi Review of Books*, *New York Journal of Books*, the *Poetry Project Newsletter*, *Current Biography*, the *Columbian*, the *Oregonian*, *Willamette Week*, the *Vancouver Voice*, the *Vancouver Vector*, and the *Boulder Planet*. His chapbooks include *tributes and ruminations* (Dristil Press, 2000), *On the Beam* (with David Madgalene, 2005), *Sketches for a Paranoid Picture Book on Memory* (King of Mice Press, 2005), and *GHOST TOWN, USA* (This is Not an Albatross, 2008).

To Be Named and Other Works of Poetic License, a poetic travelogue and art book created in collaboration with David Madgalene and Toni Lumbrazo Luna was released in July 2010, and accompanied by an art show at Angst Gallery in Vancouver, WA displaying many of the one-of-a-kind covers for the book, each of which was made by altering an album cover.

"More than we can bear," an epic investigative poem about the aftermath of September 11, was anthologized both online (*For Immediate Release*) and in print (*On the Way After 9/11*, 2002 and *Candles in the Dark, Flames for the Future*, 2003, ed. David James Randolph, New Way Media). His most recent publication is *Brutal Glints of Moonlight*, a chapbook containing poems based on Norman Mailer's 1980 Pulitzer-Prize winning novel *The Executioner's Song* for Pulitzer Remix, a National Poetry Month project sponsored by the *Found Poetry Review*.

Luna is also the author of *Literal Motion* (Bootstrap Press, 2001), which features three interviews with the filmmaker Stan Brakhage. In May 2011 Big Bridge published *The Flame Is Ours: The Letters of Stan Brakhage and Michael McClure 1961-1978,* an important piece of Twentieth-Century literary and cinema history that Luna compiled and edited at Brakhage's request.

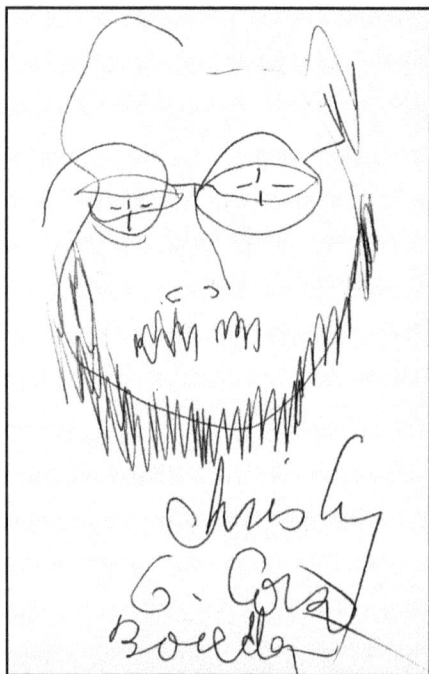

In 1994, at the Allen Ginsberg tribute Beats and Other Rebel Angels at Naropa University, Gregory Corso sketched Christopher Luna's portrait in the front of his copy of Corso's Gasoline. Christopher had asked him to sign the book, and when it seemed to be taking longer than expected, he asked the poet what he was doing. Corso replied, "You look slick. You remind me of Tennessee Williams. I'm drawing you with stars for eyes."

www.ingramcontent.com/pod-product-compliance
Lightning Source LLC
Chambersburg PA
CBHW071350090426
42738CB00012B/3075